PERFECTING THE MARCHING BAND

PERFECTING THE

MARCHING BAND

Techniques
and procedures for
marching musical units
of all sizes
by Herbert J. Gall

edited by
George S. Howard, Col. USAF (Ret.)
President, National Band Association

Abelard-Schuman
A N Intext PUBLISHER
New York   London

LIBRARY OF CONGRESS CATALOGING IN PUBLICATION DATA

Gall, Herbert J
Perfecting the marching band.

1. Marching bands. I. Title.
MT733.4.G3   785'.06'71   72-9548
ISBN 0-200-04002-2

NEW YORK   LONDON
Abelard-Schuman   Abelard-Schuman
Limited   Limited
257 Park Avenue South   450 Edgware Road
10010   W2 1EG

Published on the same day in Canada by Longman Canada Limited

Printed in the United States of America

After examining the manuscript of *Perfecting the Marching Band,* I was so impressed that I strongly encouraged the author to submit it for publication and I also requested that I be permitted to write a preface for it.

Here is a work of such value and significance to marching musical units and all activities and organizations sponsoring them that this book will ultimately be found in the library of every school possessing a band, on the desks of all organizations planning parades, and in the hands of every director and drum major heading up a band.

Sixteen years ago, Herbert J. Gall was placed under my command for the express purpose of creating the "ultimate" in marching musical units. He improved standard tactics and developed many new concepts to accomplish his mission. He built a marching musical unit for the Air Force that for years made history and was recognized both here and abroad as having no equal. It became the feature of European tattoos, thrilled millions in Scotland, Belgium, and the Middle East. It was a model for every marching band and drum corps in America.

In writing this book, he has drawn upon his experiences in organizing, training, maintaining, and supporting the world's most outstanding and proficient marching musical unit. His instructions and recommendations are detailed in terms of *techniques and procedures* that can be readily adapted. The style is firm and logical and with good continuity. All points are well made. His language is down to earth and easily understood. He discusses tips on planning formations and parade columns with the same voice of authority and experience as when he offers instructions for drum corps pageantry, for selecting uniforms, or preparing for a marching band competition. His diagrams are clear and accurate in minute detail.

My greatest contribution now to the field of music education and to all persons or organizations dealing with or maintaining marching musical units is to urge them to examine and thoroughly study *Perfecting the Marching Band.* The book is truly the encyclopedia of success for marching bands, drum corps, and committees planning parades and marching band contests.

GEORGE S. HOWARD, COL. USAF (RET.), A.B., B.M., M.M., A.M., MUS. D.
For twenty years Commander and Conductor of the
U. S. Air Force Band and Symphony Orchestra

Contents

1

The foundation
1

Chapter 1 explains in detail the fundamental concepts and techniques upon which a good marching musical unit is built.

2

Personnel
27

This chapter deals with people. Some very vital factors are discussed about the actions required of leaders and their problems in dealing with marching musicians. The levels of responsibility and authority of key individuals in the unit are explored and analyzed.

3

A study of
formation
design

55

The design of formations and maneuvers is a very large factor in the activities of a marching musical unit. This chapter discusses procedures and techniques necessary to well-planned and balanced design work. Several designs are illustrated to demonstrate the design process.

4

A study of
standard maneuvers
and formations

79

Just as a marching musical unit builds a library of music, it should also build a library of formations. Some formations and maneuvers can be classed as standards in the same way that some musical scores are classed as standards. In this chapter the composition of such standards is explained and several standard-type show pieces are illustrated.

1

The foundation

INTRODUCTION To develop a sharp-looking and precision marching musical unit with high esprit de corps is an enormous task. It is practically impossible for any one individual to carry out the assignment. First, a person would have to excel as a musician, director, arranger, tactician, strategist, personnel manager, designer, and military footwork expert. Second, there are only twenty-four hours in a day, which is not enough time for one individual to execute all of the tasks, even though he might be proficient in each one.

The most demanding and important job of the director is that of music master and overall manager. His time must not be drained away handling tasks that can be carried out by other members of his organization.

The purpose of this book is to assist the director to obtain maximum positive results with a marching unit. It deals extensively with the *nonmusical* aspects of a marching musical unit using proven procedures and techniques. *Procedures and techniques*, rather than any exact plan, are stressed, since every organization differs in size, instrumentation, purpose, and locality. These procedures and techniques can be adapted for use by any marching unit.

While the text was written primarily for marching musical units, it contains a great deal of information for nonmusical marching groups such as Scout troops and Shriners drill teams. Problems presented and analyzed were selected because they appeared as major interest areas at conferences held by the author with directors and key personnel of marching units in this country and abroad.

THE ESTABLISHED PACE AND INTERVAL The established pace and interval are requirements so basic and vital to a marching musical unit that every marching step, each formation, and all maneuvers are centered on them. There is nothing that precedes the requirement for an established pace and interval for a marching unit. The basis for the unit's marching appearance is an established pace and interval. A correct pace and interval must be calculated for each unit. They cannot be estimated; they must be computed for each individual unit.

The establishment of a correct pace and interval is not complicated. First, measure off a straight line, 100 yards in length. Second, to a simple cadence, have every member of the organization individually march the 100-yard distance at a comfortable step. Count the number of steps each member takes to march the distance. Total all the steps and then divide by the number of bandsmen who participated. Finally, divide this figure into 3,600, which is the number of inches in 100 yards, and the resulting figure will be the established pace for the unit. This pace will fall somewhere between 22 and 30 inches, depending upon the size and age of the marchers. In order to determine the correct interval, multiply the established pace by two. The correct established interval should be exactly two established paces.

EXAMPLE

Name	Number of Steps to March 100 Yards	Calculations
1. Smith	138	8,280 divided by 60 = 138
2. Jones	141	138 = average number of steps to cover 100 yards
3. Brown	136	3,600 divided by 138 = 26.0
4. White	130	26 inches = established pace of the unit
―――		52 inches = the established interval of the unit
―――		
―――		
60. Boyle	140	
TOTAL	8,280 steps	

In the example, the average pace was established at 26 inches. When the established pace is set, each member must adjust his pacing to fit. The established pace is of such importance that any means to fix it in the minds of the musicians is justified.

As an example, in the school or rehearsal hall frequently used by the members, paint, in a straight line on the floor, a series of ten two-inch circles whose centers are separated by the exact number of inches determined as the established pace; in this case, it would be 26 inches. The members can practice their pacing on these circles whenever they pass by.

Once the average pace is established, the band interval can be established. *The established interval must always be two established paces.* The only interval that will permit the proper execution of rank and file footwork and movement is a two-pace interval. It is impossible to do anything with odd intervals except cause confusion. If the band is small, do not spread it all over the street—keep it small and compact. No one will be fooled by spreading it out. In addition, it puts the unit in an impossible situation. As an example, a small drum corps may be told by the director to spread out so that the marchers assume roughly an interval of three paces in width and depth. Now, supposing it is necessary to execute a right turn when parading down the street, the men in the front rank turn by pivoting on the balls of their left feet. When the second rank comes to that line the men cannot make a right turn because they strike that particular line with their right feet instead of their left. Using an established interval of two paces, this problem would never arise. It could be said that the same turn would have worked if the interval had been four or six paces. This is correct but improbable because it is extremely difficult to hold a four-pace interval even with a seasoned, well-practiced band. A six-pace interval is simply impossible to maintain.

The established interval is the foundation of a guide system and the basis for all rank and file maintenance. Once it is established, unit members should be completely indoctrinated as to its value. Never attempt to set intervals by pacing off distances. Use a tool. The type of tool needed here is a piece of heavy stretched twine with knots indicating the established intervals. This twine can be carried by the drum major or one of the drill masters and each time the unit practices outside, the intervals in the T can be set up using the twine as a measuring device (for explanation of the T, see "A Guide System" in this chapter). By checking and rechecking the interval, the members learn exactly what is required and, furthermore, are impressed with its importance. To build anything exact and precise, it is necessary to start with precision and establish an interval of an exact dimension. The established interval is the starting point for a precise guide, which permits precision marching and maneuvering.

Once the pace and interval are established, the side step also becomes a set dimension. The side step is one half of the established pace. In the case used for an example, where the pace was established at 26 inches, the side step became 13 inches. All paces and intervals become multiples of the established pace.

THE BLOCK FORMATION The block formation is a predetermined, exact, and stable size of a marching musical unit.

The block formation is composed of the following characteristics:

1. A rectangular form for marching and maneuvering.

2. A size that can always be filled so that every rank and/or file is always complete. This means that "spare" or "utility" men must be available. A minimum of 15 percent of the total membership should be available as replacements.

3. A numerical and alphabetical designation for each position to aid in formation design and member location.

4. An established interval, both rankwise and filewise, of two established paces to permit maneuver precision.

The value of the block formation is proved in the following ways:

1. The exact size of the unit, such as six across and ten deep, will always "work" on parades or field performances. The band becomes known as, for example, a sixty-piece band, because the block of sixty is always turned out for performances.

2. With an exact dependable size, formations can be designed with no worries about vacancies. Over a period of time a fine library of good formations can be designed which may be used for years afterwards should the occasion arise. A book of standard formations, ready for use on a moment's notice, can be compiled.

3. Maximum flexibility can be achieved with an exact size because the area which the block will cover (the exact space required for maneuvers, parades, etc.) is always known.

4. The block will allow for a very exacting "guide and cover" system to be formulated. (See the section titled "A Guide System.")

With the foregoing points in mind, we shall set up a block formation for a medium-sized high school band.

The Green Valley High School has an annual band turnout averaging from 75 to 90 aspirants. The block for this band should be a sixty-man formation—six across and ten deep. The sixty-man block is the marching band that can be designated as the "first team" or the "big band." This is the band that has replacements; the band that permits a selective process enabling the director to put the most qualified bandsmen in the marching band. The remainder of the band personnel can be trainees and replacements.

Notes on the block formation

1. The nomenclature of the block is exact. Note *Diagram 1.*

2. Each position has a designation such as A3, H5, E1, and so on. This is very useful in designing formations.

3. The block should always have an even number widthwise, such as four, six, or eight; only with an even number of files can symmetrical formations be produced.

4. The block formation should have a symmetrical balance of instrumentation, which means that instruments are placed by twos. For example, when forming a sixty-member band, two snare drums added to the block should be placed in one rank, in positions one and six, or five and two, or three and four. It is a mistake to put a pair of snare drums in the same rank in files one and five because they would not be symmetrically balanced. A snare drum should not be paired with a sax or tuba because they do not balance visually (see section titled "Balance in the Marching Musical Unit"). The instrumentation to the left of center should be duplicated by the instrumentation to the right of center, in each and every rank. This produces visual balance and gives at least 85 percent of all formations perfect symmetry.

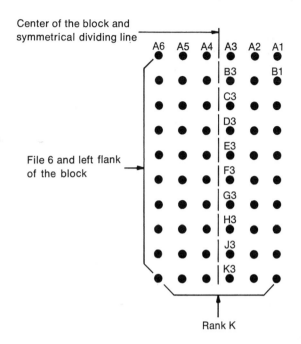

● — Drum major

Center of the block and
symmetrical dividing line

A6 A5 A4 │ A3 A2 A1
●   ●   ● │ ●   ●   ●
          │ B3   B1
●   ●   ● │ ●   ●   ●
          │ C3
●   ●   ● │ ●   ●   ●
          │ D3
●   ●   ● │ ●   ●   ●
          │ E3
●   ●   ● │ ●   ●   ●
          │ F3
●   ●   ● │ ●   ●   ●
          │ G3
●   ●   ● │ ●   ●   ●
          │ H3
●   ●   ● │ ●   ●   ●
          │ J3
●   ●   ● │ ●   ●   ●
          │ K3
●   ●   ● │ ●   ●   ●

File 6 and left flank
of the block →

Rank K

Diagram 1 / **The block formation and nomenclature** A, B, C, etc., are ranks. 1, 2, 3, etc., are files. The distance between A1 and A2 is a rank interval. The distance between A1 and B1 is a file interval. Rank and file intervals must be equal. A1 through A6 is the front rank. File 1 is the right flank. The members are A1, B1, C1, D1, E1, F1, G1, H1, J1, and K1. In this 60-man block A3 is the pacesetter.

● — Position of bandsman

The block formation is a blueprint of the marching band, standing or marching at attention, at established rank and file intervals. It codes each member's position; it is the structure into which the guide element must be inserted; it is the formation from which all field show designs and maneuver work can originate and end. In addition, the block formation is what the public sees 100 percent of the time while the unit is on parade. It is *fundamental and necessary* for any organization aspiring to higher honors to perfect the block formation.

A GUIDE SYSTEM Frequently, the total guide instruction given to bandsmen is "keep the lines even." This is not enough! A plan is necessary. A plan that details the procedures and mechanics necessary for the execution of the order.

A guide system is another of the basic factors that must be mastered by a marching unit. A good guide is one that can:

1. Control the unit under all circumstances.

2. Keep guide distances to a minimum.

3. Establish ranks widthwise, files depthwise, and angles diagonally.

4. Fix responsibility as to who does what.

A guide system that has been used under every conceivable condition, and one that has proved its value beyond all doubt, is the T system.

In order to explain the T system, we shall use a sixty-piece band whose interval has been established at 56 inches. It is of the utmost importance that the block formation, described in the preceding section, be thoroughly understood since all its designations and nomenclatures are utilized in the T guide system. The basis of this system is the letter T. It can be thought of as an imaginary T, but the function of the men in it is by no means imaginary. Note *Diagram 2*, where the T is designated by framing the guide men.

The width interval is set by the A rank—the men in the head of the T, A1, A2, A3, A4, A5, and A6. These men establish the 56-inch width interval in the front rank using A3 as the origin. These bandsmen have a twofold task:

1. To stay in line with A3.

2. To maintain a 56-inch interval on the side to which A3 is located in relation to their position. For example: A2 maintains the interval on his left, 56 inches from A3. A1 maintains the interval

Diagram 2 / **The T guide system**

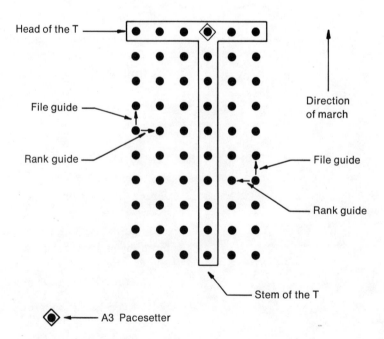

Head of the T

File guide

Rank guide

Direction of march

File guide

Rank guide

Stem of the T

Drum major

A3 Pacesetter

on his left, 56 inches from A2. A4 maintains the interval on his right, 56 inches from A3, and so on. This constitutes the head of the T.

The key figure in the T is A3, who is a member of both the head and the stem of the T. A3 sets the pace for the entire unit, and must be thoroughly trained by the drill master to maintain the established pace. In addition, it is the job of A3 to set the line of march for the unit. A3 continually marches to a distance point which he selects and *must not* guide on the drum major or any other part of the unit. He is the only completely independent figure in the T and must pay no attention to the other members of the guide T.

The guide in depth is set by the individuals in the stem of the T (file number 3), A3 through K3. These bandsmen in the stem have a twofold task:

1. To stay covered on the man or men in front of them.

2. To maintain the proper depth interval, which is always two established paces. The men in the stem of the T pay no attention whatsoever to what goes on to their right or left so far as the alignment of the men in their rank is concerned. They maintain the exact stem of the T—that is all.

This is the guide T which can, in a sense, be considered independent from the rest of the unit. Although the members of the T are a part of the unit, they must be indoctrinated to maintain the T and forget the other members, that is, they must align themselves only with the other members of the T.

Each individual in the remainder of the band, exclusive of the men in the T, has a twofold task:

1. To stay covered filewise on his guide man in the head of the T.

2. To stay covered rankwise with his guide man in the stem of the T.

Each number one and two men, in this example, will guide left while numbers four, five, and six will guide right for their rank alignment.

When the T is well set and the rest of the band is covered down, all ranks, files, and diagonals will be perfect.

The T guide system fulfills all the requirements of a good system because it can:

1. Operate under all circumstances: The T guide system, worked perfectly on hundreds of parades and field performances in the USA and abroad, has shown that it is a universally operational system. Unit members verified this in that they depended on the guide T entirely and looked upon the members of the T as specialists in the organization.

2. Provide minimum guide distances: The difficult guide to maintain is the rank guide. This system places the rank guide as near to the center as possible, thus cutting down distances for right and left guide to a minimum. The file guide is much easier to maintain and can be placed only in the front rank.

3. Establish ranks, files, and diagonals: This, as with any guide system, requires practice; however, no other system will establish better ranks, files, and diagonals with less practice.

4. Fix Responsibility: It is easy to see where the responsibility lies. A3 is responsible for the pace and linear direction of the entire unit. A1, A2, A4, A5, and A6 are responsible for the intervals between the files. B3, C3, D3, E3, F3, G3, H3, J3, and K3 are responsible for the intervals between the ranks.

Notes on "A guide system"

1. Select the T personnel as carefully as possible. Men who accept the task as a personal challenge and strive to do the best possible job should be chosen.

2. The "pacesetter" must be carefully selected and thoroughly trained—remember, he is the most important individual in the guide T.

3. Always establish the intervals in the T before the organization begins to practice. *Never set the intervals by pacing the distances. Use a measuring device.*

4. Rehearse the T alone on the field as often as possible. Get the T members acquainted with the intervals that must be maintained and impress them with the fact that as far as the guide factor is concerned, they are independent of the rest of the unit.

5. In any maneuver or formation, always designate the exact moment or point at which the guide shifts to either flank (if this shift is necessary) and also designate the moment or point at which the guide shifts back to the T. Make these shifts away from the T as few and as short in duration as possible.

6. A T will not work more effectively in a block having an odd number of files. It may appear so on paper, but I can assure you that a block having an odd number of files has a great disadvantage on formation work.

THE SIZE OF BANDS   The belief "the bigger the better" is a fallacy. Some units range in size up to 160 bandsmen. A band of such size is complete only in infrequent cases. Also, such a unit usually includes a percentage of members who are by no means qualified to be placed in any marching band. The unqualified members play and march poorly and detract from the total performance. A turnout of one hundred potential bandsmen should not necessarily mean a one-hundred piece marching band.

The idea that a ninety-six-piece band is better than a sixty-piece unit is false reasoning. A great band is one that possesses superb quality, not mass. Should there be one hundred for the marching band, the best eighty should be selected, keeping a ready reserve of twenty. Make a tight unit, that is, a unit whose size will never be in doubt and one that can operate at peak efficiency under all conditions. As a director, never be in a position where you must ask the question "How large a band will I have today?" A marching musical organization is supposed to be a showpiece, to be precise in its movements, and to play inspiring music. A program should be established whereby the band can operate at top efficiency and, simultaneously, weak members can be brought up to a standard of proficiency.

There are bands and corps of all sizes, but there are certain ideal sizes for a good marching unit. A marching unit cannot have twenty-three, forty-nine, or eighty-seven members and be balanced. In order to have visual balance, it must have a certain combination of ranks and files:

1. Twenty members—four across and five deep.

2. Twenty-four members—four across and six deep.

3. Twenty-eight members—four across and seven deep.

4. Thirty-two members—four across and eight deep.

5. Forty-two members—six across and seven deep.

6. Forty-eight members—six across and eight deep.

7. Fifty-four members—six across and nine deep.

8. Sixty members—six across and ten deep.

9. Eighty members—eight across and ten deep.

10. Ninety-six members—eight across and twelve deep.

All the factors that have been mentioned will aid either directly or indirectly in determining the size of the band. If a fine organization is desired, it is wise to forget about numbers. Build a good band of a size that can always be depended upon, with adequate replacements available, and remember, once a marching band approaches one hundred members, it is at maximum size for precision fieldwork and control while on parade.

SIGHT VERSUS SOUND   The visible aspect concerns neat uniforms, clean shoes, shined instruments, correct postures, uniform instrument positions, alignment of files, ranks and diagonals, and finally, concentration by all members on the performance. The visible considerations are based upon the fact that what a person sees is more understandable, more impressive, and more memorable than what he hears. The old expression "I'll believe it when I see it" indicates that subconsciously people place more faith in what they see than in what they hear.

Many directors forget that during a parade the general public is more aware of the spectacle than the music. A band playing simple arrangements and making a fine appearance will make a more favorable and lasting impression than a fine-sounding unit that looks bad. Remember that during a parade 90 percent of the audience reaction is triggered by what they see: the spectacle! It is a great temptation for a director to have his band play six or more marches while on parade. Unfortunately, no one along the route of march will ever know whether more than one march was used by his unit since by the time it has finished one march selection, it is usually out of ear-shot before starting another.

Regardless of a marching unit's musical proficiency, only two "solid" marches, separated by good drum cadences, should be used during a parade. These marches should be memorized and used in the line of the march so the musicians' ability is not taxed even after parading three or four miles.

Using two marches for a parade has many advantages. The director as well as the band members can devote much more time to appearance and the perfection of marching techniques. After the music has been memorized, music books are unnecessary. Attention can be paid to posture, lines, files, diagonals, and the drum major's signals. Playing on the march is difficult enough for a musician; loading him down with the additional problems of reading the music and changing the numbers compounds the difficulty. Stress the things that will impress the spectators—use ample practice time to improve the visual aspects of the unit.

A wise bandleader will work his marching band outdoors at every opportunity. He will keep two memorized marches ready at all times for a parade. When on parade, the bandsmen can put 85 percent of their attention on the appearance of the unit and still play the memorized music correctly.

Impress upon the members of the band the importance of the visual aspects and explain the reason for using two marches in a parade. Consider the visual effect of your band on parade and then schedule time to:

1. Memorize the music during indoor rehearsals.

2. Practice outside to develop files, posture, and maneuvers.

3. Combine the music and marching at outside rehearsals.

TEMPOS FOR PARADES AND FIELD PERFORMANCES

Some directors, in order to be different, use extreme tempos when their unit is performing. Even if one concurs in this thinking, tempos should be limited to the musicians' ability to execute the music properly. As the tempo of march music is raised more and more, fewer and fewer of the marching musicians can play it cleanly and the music becomes jerky and sloppy. When the tempo is too high for the band to execute the music properly, much harm is done to the bandsmen both singly and collectively. There are tempo limits for units on parade with other marchers and there are reasonable tempo limits for a unit performing alone at a football game halftime show. It is not wise for a director to exceed the tempo limits because his organization will suffer and he will look somewhat irresponsible.

Notes on parade tempos

1. The tempos within a parade column should never fall below 120 nor exceed 130 beats or steps per minute. The parade column can move fairly smoothly within these tempo limits. Great gaps and jam-ups can be avoided. It must be remembered that in addition to tempo the parade column movement is determined by the length of pace of the marchers.

2. The tempo and the length of pace factors can be largely controlled in a parade by using a unit on foot to head the parade. A marching musical unit, a military color team, or a ceremonial police marching group can do much to help keep the tempo within limits.

3. The tempo used by a band or drum corps on parade has a direct and important effect on the appearance of the marchers' posture, ranks, files, and footwork. If the tempo exceeds 130 on a long parade the appearance of the band is degraded.

4. The tempo used on a parade has a direct and important effect on the quality of the music the band produces. All directors should know that if 90 percent of their musicians can play a march cleanly at 120 steps per minute, perhaps less than 25 percent can play the same music cleanly at 140 steps per minute.

5. A tempo difference of six to ten steps per minute has a great impact on the performers in a five-mile march. Do not believe that because a drum corps looks sharp using a tempo of 136 on a ten-minute competition routine that 136 is a good parade tempo for the corps.

Notes on field performance tempos

1. The tempos for field performances can reach 136 steps per minute. This is somewhat higher than parade tempos because:
   a. The band or corps is working alone; it will not interfere with other music and/or performers.
   b. The performance time is quite short, eight to fifteen minutes and the performers do not move continually as in a parade.

2. Tempos above 136 steps per minute are acceptable for short bursts of music in a concert number or movement in a maneuver. Variation in tempos during a field performance is not only permissible but highly recommended, because it adds color and interest to the music.

3. A massing of bands on the field for some combined activity should be treated as a parade and the tempo should not exceed 130 steps per minute.

No writer should ever tell a director what tempo his marching band should use, but it is suggested that all tempos for units on the march and performing be kept within certain limits. These limits permit cooperative work with other units and permit the band to function at a high level of proficiency.

BALANCE IN THE MARCHING MUSICAL UNIT

The word "balance" signifies different things to different people. To a musician, balance means tonal balance, but a band leader must realize that musical balance alone will by no means give his unit a reputation of being a good or great marching musical organization.

When considering balance one must emphasize:

1. Visual balance of instrumentation.

2. Height or bulk balance of the members.

3. Musical balance.

In order to review thoroughly these three factors it is necessary to consider them separately:

Visual balance of instrumentation

The placement of instruments is of major importance in achieving good visual balance for the audience. During a parade one frequently sees musical units passing in which a clarinet, trumpet, or bass horn is in a rank with the trombones, drums, or piccolos. This may have been caused because an empty space had to be filled or because the unit was minus a particular instrument. It is impossible to have instrumentation balance filewise, but there is little excuse for having an unbalanced rank. One drum in a rank with five trumpets is out of balance and, no matter how unique the unit is otherwise, this placement will detract from the overall appearance. If one man is missing from a six-man line of trumpets and there is no spare trumpet man to replace the absentee, the unit would present a far better appearance by having a replacement simply hold a trumpet. Instruct him to hold it as the other trumpets are held but not to attempt to play it.

A clarinet in a drum rank or a saxophone in a tuba rank creates visual unbalance. It is essential to keep the block symmetrical—one that can be cut in half lengthwise and the right and left halves will be equal. For visual balance each rank made up of the same instruments should present a perfect picture. Unfortunately this is not always possible or practical for the following reasons:

First, an entire rank of bass drums or cymbals would look a bit ridiculous. Second, musicians who play instruments such as French horns, bassoons, and oboes are scarce.

In such cases it is necessary to make the next best visual balance by placing instruments in a rank in pairs, counterbalancing each other. An example of visual balance follows (for illustration purposes the proper intervals have been disregarded).

★
DRUM MAJOR

This			=		This
TB	TB	TB	TB	TB	TB
FH	B	B	B	B	FH
C	C	C	C	C	C
S	S	S	S	S	S
SD	SD	SD	SD	SD	SD
SD	CYM	BD	BD	CYM	SD
T	T	T	T	T	T
T	T	T	T	T	T
T	T	T	T	T	T
BH	BH	BH	BH	BH	BH

To obtain balance, there must be a reserve pool from which to select the correct replacements for absentees. There are many different arrangements of instruments, but each rank should be balanced. Note that the second rank on this plan has two French horns and four baritones, but visual balance is there. An alternative, still retaining symmetry, would be to put the French horns in the middle of the second rank in positions B3 and B4 and place the baritones on the outside of the French horns. Either placement in the block formation would achieve visual balance and would allow symmetrical formations on the field.

An unbalanced condition may be caused by poor formation design, but frequently symmetrical formations are impossible because the block formation is not symmetrical. Unbalanced formations are illustrated in *Diagram 3*. These formations would be greatly improved if the component parts were diametrically opposite each other, thus creating visual equilibrium.

Note *Diagram 4*, where the same instruments, in the same formations, are in visual equilibrium.

Bulk equilibrium of members

After achieving a visual balance of instrumentation in the unit, a further refinement can be made. Since all playing members are not the same height, it is wise to adjust the placement of different heights in the block in order to achieve the best possible bulk equilibrium. Although only a certain amount of latitude is open to the director on height adjustment, it is worthwhile to make that adjustment if it improves the appearance of the unit.

The height adjustment should be made by considering each rank as a separate element, but only after the balance of instrumentation has been accomplished. The members should be arranged in each rank according to height, using the tall men in the middle and graduating to

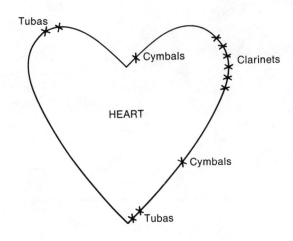

Diagram 3 / **Formations with poor visual balance** Instrumentation in the block formation is not balanced rankwise, hence balanced formations are not usually possible in symmetrical formations.

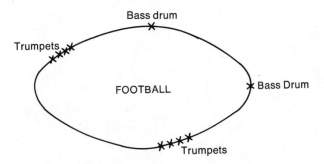

Diagram 4 / **Formations with good visual balance** Instrumentation in the block formation is balanced rankwise. This makes it possible always to balance symmetrical formations.

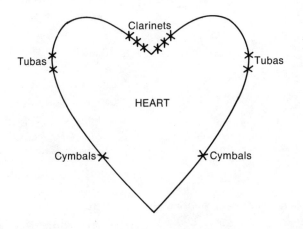

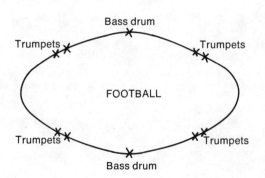

the shorter men on the flanks. If six trumpets are to be put in a rank and the heights of the men vary—six feet, one; five feet, eight; and five feet, seven—the men should be put in a rank reading across the front from left to right thusly: five feet, eight; five feet, nine; six feet, one; five feet, eleven; five feet, eight; and five feet, seven. The short members are now on the flanks, the tall members in the center. This gives bulk equilibrium in the only possible manner that it can be obtained. In a rank that is made up of different instruments the bulk equilibrium of the members problem is more difficult, but even here some degee of balance is possible. For example, in a six-man rank composed of two clarinets, two bassoons, and two alto saxophones, the two clarinets would be balanced in positions 1 and 6, or 2 and 5, or 3 and 4. If the heights of the clarinet members vary greatly there is no possibility to achieve bulk equilibrium in this particular rank because the visual balance of instrumentation must never be compromised.

The purpose of both visual instrument balance and bulk equilibrium is to present a unit appearance which, if it were separated filewise down the center and each half put on a balance scale, the scale would read zero.

Tonal or musical balance   This section deals with musical balance and here the band leader should exercise his prerogatives. Some directors prefer a preponderance of brass; some lean toward reeds and so on. The musical balance factor must rest with the band leader. It should be remembered, however, that for a musical unit that performs out of doors, the power lies with the brass and percussion.

FUNDAMENTAL FOOTWORK   No matter what type of marching unit is considered; no matter what types of parades or ceremonies are considered, one basic consideration is fundamental footwork. The development of precision in marching is predicated on the thorough mastery of fundamental footwork. In every line of endeavor certain fundamentals are paramount and unless the basic elements of an operation are well established, progress is difficult. The military has developed the required movements. Movements have been improved until they are elementary and their number has been reduced to a relative few.

Experience has shown that training in fundamental footwork has many advantages:

First, it develops coordination.

Second, it develops posture.

Third, it instills confidence and assurance.

Fourth, it proves the necessity of a chain of authority.

Fifth, it helps develop pride and an esprit de corps.

The minimum number of positions and movements required of a marching musical unit for a presentable performance follows.

1. Positions
   a. Attention
   b. Rests
   c. Facings
   d. Salutes

2. Movements
   a. Quick Time
   b. Halt
   c. Mark Time
   d. Half Step
   e. Side Step
   f. To March by the Flank
   g. To March to the Rear
   h. To March by the Half Right or Left
   i. To March Other Than at Attention

An explanation of the fundamental footwork *without* instruments follows:

1. Positions
   a. Position of the bandsmen at attention
      (1) Heels on the same line and as near each other as the conformation of the man permits.
      (2) Feet turned out equally and forming a comfortable angle.
      (3) Knees straight, without stiffness.
      (4) Hips level and drawn back slightly; body erect and resting equally on hips; chest lifted and arched; shoulders square and falling equally.
      (5) Arms hanging straight down, without stiffness, so that the thumbs are along the seams of the trousers; backs of the hands out; fingers held naturally.
      (6) Head erect and squarely to the front; chin drawn in so that the axis of the head and neck are vertical; eyes straight to the front.
      (7) Weight of the body resting equally on the heels and the balls of the feet.
   b. Rests: All rests are executed from the halt. The commands are Fall out; Rest; At ease; and Parade—Rest.
      (1) At the command "Fall out," men leave ranks but are required to remain in the immediate vicinity. They resume their places at attention at the command "Fall in."
      (2) At the command "Rest," one foot is kept in place. Neither silence nor immobility is required.
      (3) At the command "At ease," the right foot is kept in place. Silence, but not immobility, is required.
      (4) At the command of execution, "Rest," of the command "Parade—Rest," the left foot is moved smartly twelve inches to the left of the right foot, the legs are straight so that the weight of the body rests equally on both feet.

At the same time, the hands are clasped behind the back, palms to the rear, thumb and fingers of the right hand clasping the left thumb lightly; silence and immobility are maintained. This is executed only from the position of attention.

(5) To resume the position of attention from any of the rests except "Fall out," the command is "Band—Attention."

c. Facings: All facings are executed from the halt and in the cadence of quick time.

(1) To the flank: The commands are "Right (Left)— Face." After the command of execution, "Face," the movement is executed in two counts. The left heel and the right toe are raised slightly and the turn is on the right heel, assisted by a slight pressure on the ball of the left foot. The left leg is straight, without stiffness; this is done in the first count (one). The left foot is set smartly beside the right foot on the count of two. Execute "Left— Face" by turning on the left heel and the ball of the right foot in a corresponding manner.

(2) To the rear: The command is "About—Face" and the movement is executed in two counts. At the command "Face," the toe of the right foot is moved to a position touching the ground a half-shoe length to the rear and slightly to the left of the left heel, without changing the position of the left foot; the weight of the body rests mainly on the heel of the left foot; the right leg is straight, without stiffness; this is done on the first count (one). The about-face is made by turning to the right on the left heel and on the ball of the right foot and placing the right heel beside the left; this is done on the second count. In facing about, the arms are held in the normal position of attention and are not allowed to swing wide. Men are taught to experiment with the position in which they place the toe of the right foot until they have attained balance and self-assurance in execution.

d. Salutes:

(1) The command is "Hand—Salute." At the command "Salute," the right hand is raised smartly until the tip of the forefinger touches the lower part of the headdress or forehead above and slightly to the right of the right eye; thumb and fingers are extended and joined, palm down; upper arm is horizontal; forearm is inclined at 45 degrees; hand and wrist are straight; at the same time the head and eyes are turned toward the person saluted. At the termination of the salute, the hand is returned smartly in one motion to its normal position by the side. The head and eyes are turned to the front, unless already facing in that direction.

(2) Saluting distance is that distance at which recognition is easy. Usually it does not exceed twenty paces. The salute

is rendered when the person to be saluted is six paces distant or at the nearest point of approach if it is apparent that he is not going to approach to within six paces. The salute is held until the person saluted has passed or the salute is returned.

(3) At the command of execution, "Arms," of the command "Present—Arms," men who are not armed execute the hand salute. They hold the salute until the command of execution, "Arms," of the command "Order—Arms" is given. (These salutes are mentioned because they are very important elements in competition, especially for drum corps.)

2. Movements

a. Quick Time: To march forward in quick time, from a halt, the command is "Forward—March." At the word "Forward," the weight of the body is shifted to the right leg without perceptible movement. At the command "March," the step off is with the left foot and continues straight forward at the established pace without stiffness or exaggeration of movements. The arms are swung easily in their natural arcs. In a parade, quick time should be from 120 to 130 steps per minute, with about 126 being the best cadence. On a field show, quick time should not exceed 136 steps per minute.

b. Halt: the command is "Band—Halt."

(1) When marching in quick time, at the command "Halt," given as the left foot strikes the ground, the halt is executed in two counts by advancing and planting the right foot and then bringing up the left foot. (This is a very difficult movement; the unit should first be brought to Mark Time, then halted.)

(2) When executing the side step, the command "Halt" is given when the heels are together; one more side step is taken and the halt is made when the heels are next brought together.

c. Mark Time: the command is "Mark Time—March."

(1) To execute Mark Time while parading, the command must be given as the left foot strikes the ground. The next step is taken by the right foot, but when the left foot is brought forward it is placed in a position beside the right foot so that both heels are in line. The cadence is then continued by alternately raising and planting each foot without a forward motion. When the foot is raised, toes should be two inches from the ground with the shoe slanted at a 45-degree angle.

(2) To execute a mark time from a halt, the command is the same as described in c(1). In this instance the mark time begins with the left foot and continues as previously described.

(3) To execute a halt from a mark time, the command must be given as the left foot strikes the ground. Next plant the right foot and set the left smartly alongside.

d. Half Step: the command is "Half step—March." (Avoid use whenever possible—this is not an eye-appealing step.)

(1) At the command "March," steps of one-half the established pace are taken in quick time. The half step is executed in quick time only.

(2) To resume full step from half step the command is "Forward—March." The command "March" comes as the left foot strikes the ground. (The next left foot steps off with the established pace.)

e. Side Step: the commands are "Right (Left) side step— March."

(1) At the command "March," the right foot is carried one-half of the established pace to the right; the left foot is then placed beside the right, left knee straight. The cadence of quick time is continued. The side step is executed only from a halt in quick time and for short distances.

f. To March by the Flank: the flank movements in marching are an important part of such maneuvers as: column right, close interval, and extend interval. For individual or group instruction in facing to the left (right) in marching, the command is "By the left (right) flank—March."

(1) To execute a left flank while marching, the command of execution must be given as the left foot strikes the ground. When the right foot advances and strikes the ground a 90-degree turn to the left is made on the ball of the right foot. The left foot next steps out in the new direction with either a half step or full step in quick time, as the case requires.

(2) To execute a right flank while marching, the command of execution must be given as the right foot strikes the ground. When the left foot advances and strikes the ground, a 90-degree turn to the right is made on the ball of the left foot. The right foot next steps out in the new direction with either a half step or full step in quick time as the case requires.

g. To Face to the Rear when marching: the command is "To the rear—March."

(1) To execute to the rear, the command of execution must be given as the right foot strikes the ground. When the left foot is advanced and strikes the ground, a 180-degree right-about is made on the balls of both feet. Upon completion of this turn maneuver in quick-step march time, the step off is made with the left foot.

h. To March by the Half Right (Left), when marching, the command is "Right (Left) oblique—March."

(1) To execute the right oblique the command of execution

must be given when the right foot strikes the ground. When the left foot is advanced and strikes the ground, a turn of 45 degrees to the right is made on the ball of the left foot. The right foot next steps out in the new direction. (The left oblique is similarly executed, but on the alternate foot and in the opposite direction.)

   i. To March Other Than at Attention: the command is "Route step—March" or "At ease—March."

     (1) "Route step—March." At the command "March," the men are not required to maintain silence nor to march in cadence at attention.

     (2) "At ease—March." At the command "March," the men are not required to march in cadence at attention, but they are required to maintain silence.

These are the positions and movements that constitute fundamental footwork necessary to move a marching musical unit. If a drill master is interested in furthering his knowledge of this type of work he would profit from studying the "Infantry Close Order Drill Manual," obtainable from the Department of the Army

NOTE: This description was presented for drill without instruments; however, only in a few instances does the instrument interfere with the explained action. In an instance such as "Parade Rest" the drill master instructs the handling of the horns or drums in the manner which he considers most fitting for his unit. All instruments of like or similar nature must be handled identically and simultaneously.

ADVANCED FOOTWORK

After the fundamental footwork has been perfected, members can be instructed in advance footwork movements. Actually a better term would be improvised steps, because they are variations of fundamental footwork. These steps are clever and showy, but they are not absolutely essential for normal fieldwork. In the design of complex maneuvers and to achieve certain clean breaks, improvised steps are often necessary. For example, when two men marching in line or abreast find it necessary for the man on the left to go to the left flank and the man on the right to go to the right flank simultaneously on a single command, then an improvised step must be executed by one of the men. Since the ultimate in precision makes some improvised movements essential they should be considered. Following are the improvised movements, together with details on their execution.

   1. Improvised right flank while in motion. The command for this maneuver is "By the left flank—March." (This is usually a baton signal, but it can be executed in coordination with the music.) The command "March" will be given as the *left* foot strikes the ground. When the right foot is advanced, pivot 90 degrees to the right on the ball of the right foot. At the same time swing the left leg around and plant it one pace in the new direction. Step off

with the right. This movement is necessary if it is required that certain members of the unit execute left and right flanks simultaneously.

2. Improvised left flank while in motion. The command for this maneuver is "By the right flank—March." The command "March" will be given as the *right* foot strikes the ground. When the left foot is advanced, pivot 90 degrees to the left on the ball of the left foot. At the same time swing the right leg around and plant it one pace in the new direction. Step off with the left.

3. Improvised right oblique while in motion. The command for this maneuver is "Left oblique—March." The command "March" will be given as the *left* foot strikes the ground. When the right foot is advanced, pivot 45 degrees to the right on the ball of the right foot and at the same time swing the left leg around and plant it one pace in the new direction. Step off with the right. (This is similar to the improvised right flank, with the exception of the magnitude of the pivot.)

4. Improvised left oblique while in motion. The command for this maneuver is "Right oblique—March." The command "March" will be given as the *right* foot strikes the ground. When the left foot is advanced, pivot 45 degrees to the left on the ball of the left foot and at the same time swing the right leg around and plant it one pace in the new direction. Step off with the left. (This is similar to the improvised left flank, with the exception of the magnitude of the pivot.

5. Exaggerated halt. The exaggerated halt is simple but highly effective. *The unit must be at mark time.* The command is "Band —Halt." The command "Halt" must be given as the left foot strikes the ground. Plant the right foot and then throw the left foot out to the left side about twenty inches and bring it smartly in against the right foot. This halt is in cadence: "Halt—Left, 1R—2L."

6. Exaggerated mark time. A good mark-time step has so much audience appeal that it should be stressed at every practice session. It has three requirements:
a. It must be easy to execute.
b. The entire unit must execute it in the same manner.
c. All members must hold a definite spot and not drift in any direction while marking time, unless they are aligning themselves.
For showmanship, the exaggerated mark time is performed as follows: The foot is raised in a natural manner, bending the knee and inclining the foot. At the top or high mark of the step, the toe should be four inches off the ground. The heel should be ten inches off the ground because the foot is inclined. The knee should be eight inches in front of the supporting leg. The leg

and foot assume this raised position effortlessly unless forced into an unnatural position. The combination of the exaggerated mark time and the exaggerated halt is excellent to show off the training and esprit of the unit.

7. The 360-degree turn or pivot while on the march. This turn is a breathtaking maneuver, but it is very difficult and requires extensive practice. It must be rehearsed individually, slowly at first, without instruments, and then brought up to cadence. The routine must then be repeated with instruments, again slowly, and then brought up to cadence. It must be mastered individually, then as a unit. The command is "Three-sixty pivot—March." The command of execution (baton, vocal, or music cue) must be given when the right foot strikes the ground. Advance the left foot, pivot 180 degrees by turning right on the balls of both feet, then swing the right foot back and plant it one half pace behind the left foot. (At this moment the marcher is facing 180 degrees from his original facing, balanced on the balls of both feet.) Pivot 180 degrees right on the balls of both feet and step off with the left foot. This must be done in cadence, as the unit then proceeds in its original direction without interruption. (This maneuver can be used to great advantage while passing in front of a reviewing stand.)

8. The 270-degree turn or pivot while in motion. This turn is by no means a necessity because its only actual purpose is to turn the individual 90 degrees off his original line of march. It is, however, a flashy maneuver and is especially effective when used in a field show where a single column or file must make a 90-degree turn on some given point. Although the turn is made one man at a time, it is difficult to master. The command for a column to turn 90 degrees right with a 270-degree pivot is "Right two-seventy—March." The maneuver is executed on a predesig-nated spot or signal. The command of execution is given as the left foot strikes the ground; advance the right foot and pivot 270 degrees left on the ball of the right foot. At the same time, swing the left leg around and then step out in the new direction with the right foot. The first step in the new direction must be one half of an established pace, as it is impossible to take a full step or pace on this first step and retain equilibrium.

To turn 90 degrees left using the 270-degree pivot, the command is "Left two-seventy—March." The command of execution is given as the right foot strikes the ground. Advance the left foot and pivot 270 degrees on the ball of the left foot. At the same time, swing the right leg around and then step out in the new direction with the left foot. (The first step must be one half of an established pace.)

9. The triple halt. This halt is a triple version of the exaggerated halt. It can be executed correctly only from a mark-time step.

The command is "Band—Halt." The command is usually signaled by a baton. Being at mark time, the command of execution must be given on the left foot. In cadence (one) plant the right foot; (two) throw the left foot out to the left about twenty inches and then set it smartly against the right foot; (three) throw the right foot out to the right about twenty inches and set it smartly against the left foot; (four) throw the left foot out to the left about twenty inches and set it smartly against the right foot. While this is a highly effective step, it cannot be executed at a tempo above 136 steps per minute.

It might be well to emphasize again that advanced footwork is dependent upon complete mastery of fundamental footwork. Do not waste time on advanced footwork if your unit is not very proficient at fundamental footwork.

PRACTICE SUGGESTIONS The methods employed in training a marching musical organization in outdoor footwork, formation work, and music are often poorly conceived and do more harm than good. In many cases bandsmen are ready for a constructive session but no definite program of what must be accomplished has been formulated. The leader's uncertainty is transferred to the bandsmen and the result can be a 50 percent loss of accomplishment. No single phase of the *modus operandi* of a marching band is more important than the outdoor practice, and therefore it is not wise to schedule this type of rehearsal unless some very vital work is done beforehand. The following factors should be considered:

1. It is essential for the unit to have been well schooled in fundamental footwork. For example, all fundamental footwork, and later, advanced footwork, should have been demonstrated and thoroughly explained (preferably indoors). *Never expect any member of the unit to do anything until he has the mechanics of his performance rigidly fixed in his mind.*

2. It is imperative that previous indoor skull sessions have covered such items as the guide system, block formation, new formations to be practiced, drum major's signals, and so forth. A good drill master will never attempt to explain basic concepts of new shows for the first time, outside, because of all the disturbing factors and lack of visual or training aids.

3. A critique of the units most noticeable outdoor weakness should be made. This should be a general critique, not aimed at individuals. An outdoor practice session might be programmed along the lines of the following format:

First: Spend five minutes practicing footwork without music. Include all of the fundamental footwork that can be executed without marching, such as right face, left face, parade rest, etc. Give the block formation a rapid series of verbal commands which cover all the positions.

Second: Spend the next ten minutes on marching footwork without music. The block formation works under the drum major's baton for the practice of forwards and halt, right and left turns, box reverses, open and close marches, mark time, and halts.

Third: Spend the next ten minutes repeating the foregoing procedure with music. One or two of the memorized marches can be used. Music that must be read should not be used while marching. At this point, the unit should be warmed up and settled down to work.

Fourth: Spend ten minutes in running through the standard formations such as company fronts, waltzes, the show start trade mark, etc. The standard formations are showpieces that should be able to be used on a moment's notice; therefore, they should be kept sharp. (See section "Standard Maneuvers and Formations" in Chapter 4.)

Fifth: Finally practice, for a maximum of fifty or sixty minutes, the new formations and maneuvers that have been thoroughly covered in skull sessions. The band should be led through the new work without music until the footwork positions and the lines of the new formations are acceptable. It should then be practiced with the memorized music. If, during this part of the practice, some of the new music to be used has not been memorized, the new formations should be practiced without music. Marching musicians cannot read music and concentrate on new footwork at the same time.

Aside from the overall plan for the outdoor practice, there are several important items that must be considered:

1. The drum major's task

   Indoor sessions will enable the drum major to explain and demonstrate baton signals. During outdoor practice the drum major should run through all of his baton signals repeatedly to give him practice and confidence. If he is uncertain, the band will be uncertain.

2. The guide system

   At all possible practices the guide T should be rehearsed alone. Here is an opportunity to impress on the men in the T that they form an independent guide system within the band and that the system sets up the gridwork on which the other members must guide. There is no change whatsoever in their task when the block is formed around them; the men in the T are the key to the guide system, completely independent of the other members in the band.

   Exact spacing and covering in the T are imperative. Intervals cannot be correctly fixed by the drum major pacing them off. A strong piece of twine, about ten feet longer than the stem of the T, stretched and knotted at the established interval distances, permits the exact spacings to be set quickly. Two of the nonmarching members can use this twine to set the exact established interval in both the stem and the head of the T. This twine should be carried at all times and should be used each time the organization practices outdoors.

3. Outdoor music

   When the unit is practicing, parading, or maneuvering it is important that the music be memorized. Nothing must divert the bandsmen's attention from their footwork, linework, and formation work.

4. Replacement personnel

   It is wise to use as many trainees as possible during training and rehearsal periods in order to indoctrinate them for the time when they will receive a permanent position in the marching band or be needed to fill a space temporarily. The best trainees should be considered "utility" personnel and should be used as replacements. Adequate grooming of the utility men is important. Let us use two clarinetists as an example: Imagine them to be two extras or trainees for the clarinet section. Every time the unit is practicing, these two extras should march in the clarinet section. Should any clarinet men be absent for a rehearsal, the extras can fill the positions. So long as the two men are extras, they should be shifted from one position to another in the clarinet section. This practice should apply to all the extras as they require both intensive and extensive practice within the block. Naturally, during a dress rehearsal the entire first team should be utilized with the extras standing by to be used only in an emergency. Such training will create a pool of ready reserves for the unit and make it possible to maintain a complete and balanced block formation at all times.

5. Skull session

   This item is not an outdoor task, but it ties in so closely with outside work that it bears mention. A classroom skull session with the entire unit, prior to outside practice, is one facet that is sometimes overlooked. This is a serious mistake. Every time a new formation or maneuver requiring footwork is to be used, the first item on the agenda should be a skull session. The session is used to explain to the personnel exactly what is expected of them at the outside rehearsal. The members should be given the overall picture before showering them with details. It is good procedure to have a complete drawing on a large blackboard, showing in detail the maneuvers to be practiced. Mimeographed copies of the maneuvers should be distributed to each member of the band. Each member should have a complete maneuver and formation folder that is controlled in the same manner as the music folder.

6. The tape recorder

   Using a tape recorder can assist in solving many problems.

a. A problem section in many bands is the percussion. It is difficult for a drummer to memorize his music unless he plays it again and again with the band. When the band has mastered a new piece of music it should be put on tape. The drummers can work as a section using the recorder instead of the band. This type of rehearsal need not be limited to the drummers; other sections, such as the second trombones or first tenor bugles, can also profit by working with the recorder.

b. New members entering the organization can use the machine to great advantage. They can play their assigned parts repeatedly with the recorder. It is also an excellent device for teaching new members standard formation and maneuver music that must be memorized.

c. The entire band can obtain much useful information from listening to a tape recording of their work. The tape is a completely unbiased critic. The instructor can easily point out weak spots and mistakes to the group.

d. The recorder can be invaluable in helping to polish a field show. After the footwork and maneuvers of the field show have been walked through several times, the entire routine can be practiced to the exact show music previously taped indoors.

7. Visual aids

The use of a movie film for training has additional advantages for the band and serves as another unbiased critic just as it does for football teams. Great use can be made of movies to aid in training the unit for outside work. It emphasizes items of general and individual interest, such as drum major signals, fundamental footwork, advanced footwork, and proper instrument positions. These are only a few of the possibilities. For example:

a. A film of the drum major could show each of the signals he uses to guide the band. A film such as this, with the proper explanation by the drum major or the director, will make lasting impressions on the bandsmen.

b. A film demonstrating the guide system will show the T and how the rank and file intervals are maintained.

c. A film shot of the unit while it is actually performing is good for morale and, in addition, can serve as a critique of actual operations.

d. A film of contest performances by the band makes excellent study material.

THE PERSONALITY FACTOR Marching units are made up of people with varied interests as well as diversified backgrounds and personalities. The leader's degree of success will depend upon his technical knowledge and how well he manages his personnel. It will further depend upon his personality. He must recognize that there is a constant interplay between his own personality and the varied ones of his charges.

A director may study and master all the techniques of his profession but this will not assure his success when he goes into action. It is a combination of knowledge plus his manner of implementation that will measure the degree of success. His manner of dealing with his personnel and watching ever so closely the delicate mechanism of human relations will determine whether or not he will successfully apply his technical knowledge.

Since one group of individuals will be better motivated by one approach than another, a good manager will endeavor to find the most effective approach. Even in a small organization, some members will respond best to a direct order while others may require only a suggestion.

Details on how to motivate a group will be of little aid, since every approach must be built around the director. Many directors attempt to emulate someone they consider to be highly successful. They usually fail to achieve comparable results, because they forget that their personality does not coincide with the personality of their hero. No two persons have the same personality, so when one attempts to copy *exactly* the methods of another, he often is in for a rude awakening. He fails to realize that the methods he may have admired were actually built around another personality, different from his own.

The leader's personality will have a strong effect upon the people he manages. This is true in any type of organization. A strong personality will be highly effective, but "strong" does not necessarily mean "a tiger." Many leaders achieve great success by operating in a mild-mannered fashion.

It is important that leaders recognize their own strengths and weaknesses and tailor their methods to them. Those who do so will greatly increase their percentage of success.

A CONCEPT OF LEADERSHIP There are three key factors which a leader must recognize and handle in a sensible and complete manner if he desires to build a noteworthy organization. These key factors are:

1. Planning

2. Organizing

3. Controlling

It matters little whether the problems be those of an entrepreneur of a great industry, or the problems of a director of a drum and bugle corps, these factors still apply. Although the terms plan, organize, and control are defined in any dictionary, it may be well to relate them to marching musical units.

1. Planning. Whenever a problem arises that does not demand an instantaneous solution, the first step is to plan. In most cases a director will have a certain amount of time to think about a problem. This interim period gives him an opportunity to formulate a solution and an implementation method. In the initial phases of planning there are two intangibles he must consider:
   a. How will his plan affect his band members and others?
   b. How will his band members and others affect his plan?

The profound meaning of these two questions should not be underestimated.

The size of the problem and its uniqueness determine the amount of planning necessary. To plan an outside rehearsal by no means necessitates the same output as planning a ten-minute contest performance. In the planning, a leader should always be willing to weigh the advice offered by the drill master, the assistant director, and others. He should end the planning when he is convinced that the plan is sound and workable. A great danger in planning is that of allowing the overall or master plan to become fogged and obscure because of untimely attention to details. When an idea is conceived or a problem is presented, the planning should first be confined to the general scheme of the operation. Too often key personnel will become entangled in trying to work out the details before they understand the route which they will take to reach the objective. In all instances the master plan format should be complete before the details are filled in. For example, a complete new field show with music must be envisioned before attacking music arangements and footwork. An overall plan should be formulated which will identify such items as:

a. Starting formation

b. Maneuver #1

c. Formation #1

d. Formation #2

e. Special concert formation and music

f. The exit

Into this must be inserted such items as time elements, distances involved, facing of audience, etc. After the basic plan is formulated, the insertion of smaller details can be undertaken. One frequently finds that as the details are inserted, some changes in the original overall plan become necessary. Planning should not be along rigid and inflexible lines where mistakes are camouflaged, not corrected; and weak spots are endured, not strengthened.

2. Organization. To put any plan into effect, a manager organizes the elements of his unit to handle the implementation, testing, and operation of the plan. A good organization structure with very definite assigned lines of authority and responsibility is essential.

3. Control. To test the true value of any plan, certain personnel and technical aspects must be monitored. There must be systematic control through a chain of command. (The chain of command is discussed in detail later in the text.)

It is unwise to assume that a man is a good leader because he is a good arranger and/or musical director. If he has no more to offer than that he is a technician. To fill the requirements of true leadership, one must be a generalist, in addition to being a specialist in one's particular field. This means that a leader must be familiar with the total operation, including the tangible aspects, such as money matters, and the intangible matters such as human personalities. Leaders are not born. Leaders are forged, to a great degree, by swinging the forging hammer for themselves. Such hammers as "understanding," "experience," "initiative," "flexibility," and the like are indispensable.

Each man has had occasions to notice that sometimes he has solved problems very smoothly and at other times very badly. He should review these instances in his own mind and attempt to analyze why one solution was good and the other was bad. If he goes through these reviews, he will begin to recognize his most effective approaches in dealing with problems. A rather common characteristic of men who are successful leaders is a continual problem resolution analysis.

In considering leaders and potential leaders who are well indoctrinated in the use of the principles of planning, organizing, and controlling, it is possible to estimate the percentage of success of each by considering the breakdown of *certain fact, determinable fact,* and *pure chance.* The first two, certain fact and determinable fact, are strictly within the control powers of the person; the third, pure chance, usually lies outside his control. For example, a leader is faced with an operational problem such as a complete reorganization of the existing marching band to make it more flexible and maneuverable, and to make it less costly to the sponsors. The leader begins with about 40 percent of the entire solution available, provided he uses his own education and experience to the fullest. This is the *certain* factor. The next

30 percent of the solution can be determined by hard work, research into what others have done, balancing one group of alternatives against another, experimentation to ascertain the value of a certain idea, etc. This is the *determinable* factor. The last 30 percent of the solution depends on lady luck, because it is impossible to ascertain with perfect assuredness what conditions will be born or what changes will come in the future, at the time when the scheme will be put into effect. Seventy percent is just about the most a good leader can donate to the success of a plan. However, if the 70 percent is worked out to the fullest extent, the idea that the project will be successful only seven out of ten times is not valid. The chance factor does not operate that harshly. In fact, considering funds as chance items, the chance factor will usually be favorable if the full 70 percent of certain and determinable facts has been worked out. There are more failures than necessary because few persons expend the energy and time to complete the full 70 percent. It is hard work and time-consuming, especially the 30 percent factor of determinables. When the full 70 percent of certain and determinable factors is not resolved, more is left to chance and thus a greater possibility of failure is created.

A leader who attacks problems with the initiative to take the determinables out of the chance category, and who plans, organizes, and controls with flexibility, will do a good job and score his share of successes. Many times the statement is made that an organization is so efficient it could run without its leaders. Nothing could be further from the truth. Such an organization is efficient because of the caliber of the leader and key personnel. This applies to marching musical units as well as to a farmers' cooperative. The degree of success of the operation is dependent on the caliber and effort of the leader and key personnel.

A good leader formulates good ideas, effectively coordinates the activities of his subordinates, and inspires his men to achieve the goals he sets for the organization. Eminently desirable is the ability to master the art of gaining acceptance from one's charges—acceptance as their guide and mentor, as well as respect for one's judgment on personnel issues. The effort necessary to achieve this ultimate goal is well worthwhile. To instill inspiration, one must never lose sight of the fact that power *with* an organization is much more important and smoother than power over an organization.

Any person acting in the capacity of a leader should read several of the excellent works published on leadership and management. Although not specifically aimed at music directors and key personnel in the marching musical field, their application is universal.

THE CHAIN OF COMMAND   To many the term "chain of command" brings to mind a rigid military-oriented "order and execute" atmosphere. Many stories attempt to discredit the theory behind the idea, but a rather strange fact appears. The dissenters never complain about the chain of command below their position; it is always that portion above their station that is at fault. This indicates that there is nothing really wrong with the system but that individuals tend to complain about not getting their own way.

The term chain of command should be construed to mean a controlled system of planning and executing action which fixes responsibility and delegates authority in a manner that will handle all contingencies. It is necessary in marching musical units. If there is no chain of command it is impossible to fix authority and responsibility and there is, consequently, general confusion. Many directors make the error of not clarifying the command line of their organizations. As a result they struggle to keep peace in the unit and must do additional work to accomplish their goals. If no command line is drawn, the drum major may give one command and the drill master another. Who should be obeyed? Examples could be given ad infinitum—everyone is familiar with the problem.

A chain of command for a marching musical unit that will handle all contingencies is illustrated in Diagram 5.

Of course, any chain must be constructed with all the factors of a particular organization in mind. The example in Diagram 5 is a very general one. In order to realize its value, it is necessary to examine each link.

1. The Director

The director in this sense is more than the musical director of the unit. He is the final word on any procedure of training or performance. His task is largely one of coordination of all the factors. He also has the task of making policy. He must formulate the rules of operation for the organization. He should consider all the ideas and respective

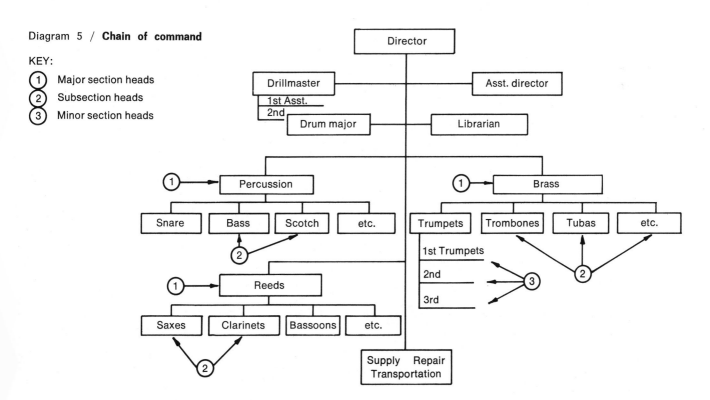

Diagram 5 / **Chain of command**

KEY:

1 Major section heads
2 Subsection heads
3 Minor section heads

wishes presented by his staff and formulate the most workable policy. The subordinate leaders should then develop the policy for their areas of responsibility. Subordinate leader policy must support the director's policies. In solving operational problems and disagreements, the director should never interfere with a section leader unless:

a. Overall policy is violated.

b. The section leader cannot satisfactorily resolve the problem.

If the leader does not allow his assistants to resolve their particular problems, he places them in a disadvantageous position by giving the impression to the band members that his staff assistants are incompetent. This voids their usefulness. If, for example, a drummer comes to the director with a problem concerning the percussion section, the director should take no action other than to send the man to the head of the percussion section. This does not have to be done often before no future attempts at breaking the chain of command will be made. Once the staff assistant realizes that his position and decisions are respected he will repay the director by increased work and loyalty.

Any grievance the director encounters that must be settled with a subordinate leader should be resolved in strict privacy. Anytime there are congratulations, they should be given in front of the entire organization. (Much has been written on the fallacy of criticizing a man in front of the men over whom he is in charge. It can cause more damage in two minutes than can be corrected in two months.)

The director has the final word. He should use tact, diplomacy, and consideration in his role. He should make certain that he is not meddling in something his subordinate leaders could adequately handle.

2. The Assistant Director

The assistant director can be concerned almost entirely with music. The only time he should act as the final authority is in the absence of the director, but his decisions must always be based on the director's policy. If a problem of a serious nature should arise during the director's absence, it should be tabled until the director returns. When the director is present, the assistant director should not be considered a part of the chain of command unless the director himself so desires and informs the group accordingly.

3. The Drill Master

Beginning with the drill master, the chain of command becomes a sectionalized affair and from this point forward continues as such. Although the drill master may be considered second in command on outside work, not all problems must go through him to reach the director. For example, any unsolvable musical problem encountered by a section head should go to the director, bypassing the drill master, whose task deals with design work, formations, maneuvers, footwork, uniforms, etc.

4. Assistant Drill Masters

Assistant drill masters should be designated as first, second, third, and so on, in order to clarify the position of drill master should the first drill master be absent. When the drill master is present the chain of command does not include the assistants unless the drill master so desires. Obviously, the reason for this is to have one and only one person in charge of a given operation at a given time.

5. The Drum Major

The drum major holds the unique position of sometimes being the supreme commander of the organization and at other times an assistant drill master, or on still other occasions, merely an observer. During indoor or outdoor music rehearsals under the director, he assumes the role of an observer and student. When the organization is broken up for sectionalized maneuver, formation, or footwork practice, he assumes the role of an assistant drill master. However, when the entire unit is working together under his baton, either at practice or on a performance, he is the commander. The drum major should have direct access to either the director or the drill master at all times.

6. The Section Heads

The major, sub, and minor section heads monitor smaller groups. They are key personnel responsible to the director and drill master for all the music and footwork of the men in their respective sections. In case of a musical problem, the direct channel is to the director. For military or footwork problems, the channel leads directly to the drill master. It is impossible to list the exact number of section heads required for an organization unless the number of members, the instrumentation, and the voicing of the instrumentation are known. The following general rules apply for all situations.

a. Each major section must have a section head. An example is the man in charge of the entire brass section.

b. Each subsection must have a section head. An example of this is the man in charge of the trumpets in the brass section.

c. Each minor section must have a section head. An example would be the man in charge of the first trumpets in the trumpet section. In the minor sections, even though there are only two members, one should be the section head.

An important factor of concern to the director is the selection of the correct person to fill each position of authority in his chain of command. This selection is vitally important because these men actually represent him and are an extension of his authority.

The director should also appoint a staff to assist him. The staff should be composed of select key men in the chain of command. When meeting with his staff, the director should encourage ideas and discussions concerning problems of the unit. It is well to limit the staff to approximately five members who are familiar with every activity of the organization. When necessary this staff can act as a research team or planning group; with the proper guidance it can also be the discipline board for the unit and recommend discipline measures to the director.

The chain of command is the network through which a large organization is controlled. It may carry other names under different conditions but it is the same thing; large companies have vast organization charts that show their command lines quite clearly.

The necessity of a chain of command or organization structure has been proved many times by management studies. The studies all agree that no one person can supervise directly and properly more than six to eight men. Note, in Diagram 5, the director retains direct supervision over eight men: the drum major, drill master, assistant director, librarian, brass section head, reed section head, percussion section head, and chief of supply.

THE DRUM MAJOR AND HIS SIGNALS

When the organization is marching as a unit the most important single individual present is the drum major. The entire marching group is dependent upon his commands. His orders must be clear, concise, forceful, and visible to all the bandsmen. A unit can be placed in an impossible situation by an untrained or indecisive drum major. He can do more damage in one minute than can be rectified in sixty. He can cause:

1. Bad step-offs, where the unit seems to stretch to almost twice its normal length before it resumes concordant movement.

2. Bad halts, where the unit jams up and comes to an "accordion stop."

3. Poor turns, where the flank of the band is run up on the sidewalk or into the bleachers.

4. Poor musical beginnings, where the organization plays eight to twelve bars before the ensemble is unified.

5. Confusion with poor baton work, where unified response is not obtained.

Many directors use detailed tests to ascertain the proper placement of musicians in order to establish musical balance. These same directors may select a drum major by saying "Joe is the tallest; therefore, he will be the drum major." In the entire process of placing men in a marching musical unit no one factor should be weighed more heavily than the drum major's position.

More important than choosing the tallest member as drum major is the selection of a person who is intelligent; one who can predetermine situations and meet them with the best possible solutions. If intelligence combined with commanding height can be found in the organization then the selection is a simple matter; but if one element must be sacrificed, height should be the one. An intelligent drum major who stands five feet, eight inches, and has good baton technique can guide a unit, whereas one who stands six feet, six inches, and has poor judgment cannot. The qualifications of a good drum major are as follows:

1. Have a high degree of intelligence. This is essential because no matter how well trained the drum major may be, he will often be confronted with situations which he alone must resolve. It is impossible to brief him on everything that may happen during a parade or field performance. Unforeseen things may occur, for which he must devise tactics to meet the situation.

2. Have some aggressiveness. If the drum major has an inert temperament, he will affect the unit with it. Any person who holds a drum

major's position must be somewhat aggressive to accomplish a task requiring boldness.

3. Have sufficient initiative. In order to handle any job of responsibility, one must have initiative to carry out his assignment and infect his co-workers with this spirit. A drum major is no exception.

4. Have good military bearing. When the unit is parading or performing, the drum major is usually occupying a center-stage position, which automatically attracts attention. As a result, he should walk and stand properly. A certain amount of prance may add brilliance but too much becomes ridiculous.

5. Have a very good memory for tempos, cues, cutoffs, signals, etc. A mistake often made in selecting a drum major is a supposition that he must be a fine musician. A great drum major of a world-famous unit was at one time a poor drummer but he had all the other qualifications necessary for the position. He listened to the music, knew every maneuver and step that had to be performed, and used a system of signals that was simple and exact. Such a person can be trained to be a top-notch drum major.

6. Be approximately six feet tall. A tall drum major is a great asset if he possesses the other necessary attributes.

The drum major's signals   A complaint frequently cited by bandsmen is that baton signals are indefinite or that the drum major has two or more signals for the same command. (One drum major boasted that he used approximately sixty different signals to guide his band. It is ridiculous to employ this many signals. They only add confusion.)

A marching band can perform very efficiently under the guidance of a drum major who uses a limited number of signals; actually, the fewer the better. The commands necessary to guide a marching musical unit under any conditions follow:

1. Assemble the Band. To assemble the block formation when the members are scattered, both a verbal command and baton signal can be used. The verbal command is "Fall In." For the baton signal, the baton is held high overhead pointing to the sky and moved in a circular motion as though drawing circles in the air with the tip. To assemble the band, the drum major should always select an open space, large enough to form the block. It should be done without crowding some members into automobiles, buildings, or ditches. The author prefers to have the guide T fall in and then assemble the unit around the T. See *Diagram 6* for the assembly signal.

2. Cover. To have the unit align itself when assembled, the drum major uses the verbal command "Cover" or "Cover down." The guide T assumes its exact spacing and alignment; the remainder of the unit covers on the head and stem of the T. This will establish the ranks, files, and diagonals.

3. Forward March—No Music. To have the band move forward without music, the command can be either verbal or a baton signal. As the unit stands at attention the drum major will command, "Forward—March." At this time the unit steps off to a single drum tap or

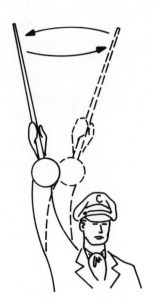

Diagram 6 / **Assembly signal** 1. There is no preparatory signal, this is the signal of execution, commanding the personnel to form the marching unit. 2. The drum major selects the area on which he desires the unit to form, faces it and uses the high circular baton motion illustrated. A well disciplined unit does not need a whistle. 3. He stands six feet in front of the position he has selected for the pacesetter in the guide T.

drum cadence. For the baton command, the drum major faces the band and instructs the men they will move forward on a drum cadence. He then faces the direction of march and holding his baton high overhead, he moves it—left, right, and down—to the tempo he wishes to establish. The left movement of the baton can be translated to mean "Forward"; the right movement to mean "March"; and the downward movement to mean "Step off." The drum major should be sufficiently forceful to make certain he has the undivided attention of the entire organization before commanding "Forward—March" or the step-off will be ragged. See Diagram 7.

4. Forward March—with Music. When the organization is assembled and standing at attention, but not playing, the drum major must inform the members verbally that they will step off to music. He must

Diagram 7 / **Forward march** 1. Signal of preparation: This is the first phase of the signal. The drum major has given the unit its instructions and assumed a position six to twelve paces in front of the band facing the direction of march. The raised baton indicates the signal of execution will follow in about six seconds. 2. Signal of execution: This is the second phase of the signal. Baton movements A and B set the tempo and the unit steps off on the C movement with or without music as previously ordered. The drum major is facing the direction of march and steps off on the C movement of the baton.

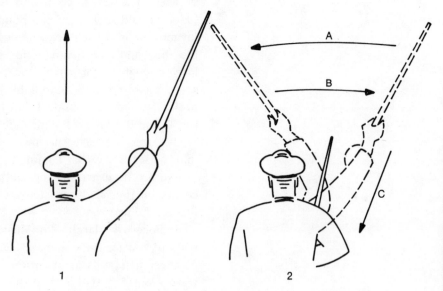

1   2

also inform the members what music will be rendered. He should ascertain he has undivided attention while giving these instructions. The baton signal to step off with music is the same as the baton signal "Forward—March" without music. (If the unit is standing at attention playing music, and the drum major desires to have the band move forward and continue to play, he uses the same action and baton signal just described for "Forward March with Music." This order cannot be confused with a music cutoff because the drum major has his back to the organization as he gives the signal. See *Diagram 7.*)

5. Mark Time. To bring the corps or band to a mark-time step, the verbal command is "Mark time—March." If the unit is moving forward on a drum tap, the drum major must turn and face the unit (which means that he will be marching backward). The word "March" is barked out as the left foot strikes the ground. The right foot is then advanced one pace and the left foot is brought up beside it in a mark-time step. If the unit is marching and playing music, the drum major faces the organization and holds the baton horizontally, high overhead, with a hand grasping either end. This serves to inform the members that they will be brought to a mark-time step but continue to play. When the drum major has the attention of the band, the baton motion is back—forward (right foot—left foot) in a one—two count. After the signal is given the right foot is advanced one pace, then the left foot brought alongside it in a mark-time step. See *Diagram 8.*

NOTE: A marching musical unit should always be brought to a mark time, then halted; it should never be halted from a forward movement.

6. Halt from a Mark-Time Step. To halt the unit from a mark-time step the command can be either verbal or by baton signal. If there is no music the verbal command is "Band or Corps—Halt." The word "Halt" is barked out as the left foot strikes the ground. The members take another mark-time step with the right foot and then set the left foot smartly beside the right. If the unit is marking time and play-

Diagram 8 / **Mark time** 1. Signal of preparation: This is the first phase of the command. The drum major is marching backward facing the unit with the baton overhead in the position shown. The preparatory signal is held approximately six seconds before the command of execution is given. 2. Signal of execution: This is the second phase of the command. This is a side view of the drum major which shows the execution movement of the baton. Actually the drum major is facing the unit. Command of execution is on left foot.

1

2

ing music, the baton signal for the halt is absolutely necessary. The drum major faces the unit with the baton held horizontally, high overhead, with a hand grasping each end. (Since the unit is already marking time this serves to inform the members that they will be halted.) When the drum major has the attention of the unit, he snaps the baton down to his waist as the left foot strikes the ground and the "halt" is executed as in the verbal command, with the music continuing. See *Diagram 9*.

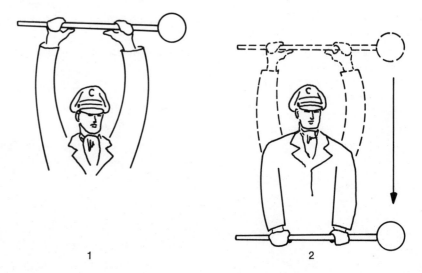

Diagram 9 / **Halting the mark time**   1. Signal of preparation: This is the first phase of the command. Drum major is facing the unit, all are marking time. The preparatory signal is held for six seconds or until the drum major notes that the unit is aligned. 2. Signal of execution: This is the second phase of the command. The execution signal is as illustrated. Command of execution is on the left foot. **Always bring the marching unit to mark time, give the members time to align themselves, and then halt the mark time.**

1   2

7. Music Cut. To stop the music, the drum major should always use a baton signal. If the unit is standing at attention, playing music, the drum major faces the band with his baton high overhead, pointing to the sky. When he has the attention of the members, he moves the baton left, right, and down. These movements mean one—two—stop. He should time the cutoff with a phrase ending in the music, but if the unit is well trained and he is forceful he can cut the music at any point. If the unit is moving along and the occasion arises when it becomes necessary to cut the music and continue to march, the drum major marches backward facing the unit with baton high overhead. He uses the alert signal (see Diagram 17) to get the unit's attention and signals for a music cut while marching backward. The unit will recognize that the signal is not one to halt the forward movement because that requires the mark-time signal. The music is cut, the unit continues its march, and the drum major turns front and continues his pace. See *Diagram 10*. The most precise manner in which to execute any music cut while on the march is a series of signals. Bring the unit to mark time; halt the mark time and finally cut the music. With diligent practice this series of three signals can be enacted in five seconds.

8. Turns. The footwork is explained in Chapter 1 in the section titled "Fundamental Footwork." The command of execution for a left turn is given on the left foot; for a right turn on the right foot; and for an oblique turn on the foot corresponding to the direction of turn. To have the unit execute a right turn, left turn, or an oblique turn by

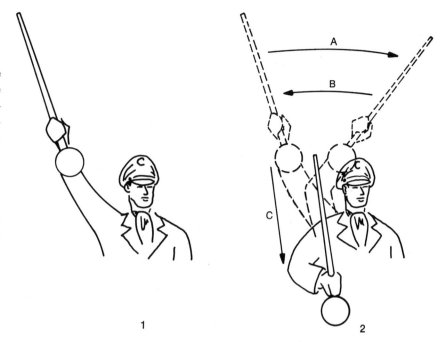

Diagram 10 / **Music cut** 1. Signal of preparation: This is the first phase of the command. The drum major is facing the unit, all are at attention, the unit is playing. The preparatory signal is as illustrated. The drum major should hold this position for at least six seconds. If the unit is moving, the drum major is marching backward. 2. Signal of execution: This is the second phase of the command. The drum major is facing the unit. The A-B-C- motion of the baton is coordinated with the music or can be thought of as left-right-left, respectively. If the unit is moving the drum major is marching backward. After the music cut he turns 180 degrees and continues the line of march.

baton, the drum major uses a set of signals that can be classified as the "turn group." To have the unit execute a right turn, either while playing music or not, the drum major, facing front or with his back to his unit, holds his baton high overhead with one hand, the baton horizontal to the ground, and the tip pointing in the turn direction (in this case, right). The baton should be in this position for at least ten steps in order to attract the attention of each member. When the front rank of the band is in the required position the baton is jabbed right with a definite motion as the right foot strikes the ground. If the unit is to make a left turn, the procedure for the drum major is the same except that the baton points left and the command of execution is on the left foot (note *Diagram 11*). For acute-angle turns or half turns the

Diagram 11 / **Right turn** 1. Signal of preparation: This is the first phase of the command. The drum major predetermines exactly where he will turn the unit. The preparatory signal should be held at least six seconds. 2. Signal of execution: This is the second phase of the command. The drum major is marching in front of the band and at the predetermined point gives the execution signal as illustrated. The command of execution comes as the right foot strikes the ground.

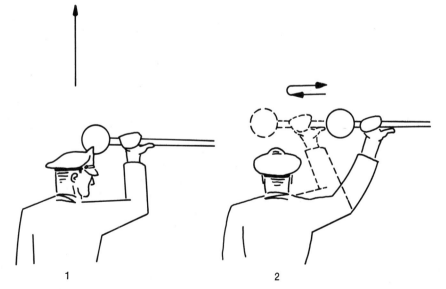

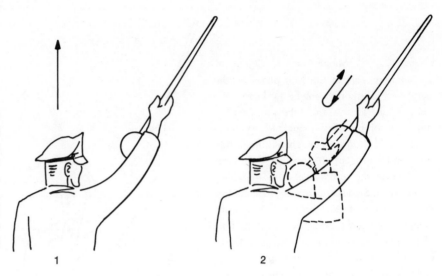

Diagram 12 / **Half right or acute right-angle turn** 1. Signal of preparation: This is the first phase of the command. The drum major predetermines the exact point at which he will turn the unit. The preparatory signal is held at least six seconds. 2. Signal of execution: This is the second phase of the command. The drum major gives the signal of execution as illustrated at the predetermined point.

1   2

procedure is the same except that the baton points about 45 degrees right or left, as necessary. *Diagram 12*, showing the acute-angle turn signal, may give the impression that it is the preparatory signal to start or stop the music, but this is not the case for two reasons:

First: In the start or stop music signal the baton is in a plane with the drum major's body. In the case of the turn the baton is angled out from the drum major's body.

Second: In the start or stop music signal the drum major is looking straight forward while in this case he faces the direction of the coming turn.

9. The Different Halts. The various halt possibilities are many: to halt the forward movement and continue to play; to halt the forward movement and cut the music simultaneously; to accomplish these things from the mark time, etc. Nevertheless, a halt under any possible condition can be accomplished by *one simple series of signals*. The band members must be made to understand that each signal means only one thing and that they must react properly to each signal. For example, if the unit is moving—playing music or not—the first signal is to bring it to a mark time, then it can be halted from the mark-time step. Finally, if music is being played, it can be cut.

Halt Sequence:

First, bring the unit to mark time.

Second, halt the mark-time step.

Third, cut the music.

This sequence has a short time element. It is a performance that requires only a few seconds, and each signal means one definite thing to the musicians. It is wise to command the unit to cease its forward motion by first bringing it to a mark-time step. If the members are brought to a mark-time step first, they can align themselves in a few seconds, then the drum major can halt the mark time. The secret is to cut down the overall number of signals and eliminate confusion for any halt combination. The key to this secret is a series of familiar baton signals, each representing only one command; not a combination of commands.

10. Countermarch or Box Reverse. The signal to execute the box reverse or countermarch should be distinctive. Since either of these maneuvers reverses the direction of march (turning it 180 degrees), one is sufficient. The baton signal is as follows: the drum major, facing the unit and moving backward as it is approaching him, holds the baton high overhead, pointed straight up, with the ball end or heavy end in the air. If properly indoctrinated and trained, the band knows immediately that the signal will be for a reverse. After seeing that he has the attention of his unit, the drum major can give the execution command for the box reverse. The baton is lowered about a foot, and raised in cadence, one—two. The count for this command is one—right foot, and two—left foot. See *Diagram 13*.

Diagram 13 / **180-degree direction change in marching** 1. Signal of preparation: This is the first phase of the command. The drum major has predetermined the exact line where the 180-degree change in the direction of march is to take place. The drum major faces the unit as it approaches him. The preparatory signal should be held for at least six seconds. 2. Signal of execution: This is the second phase of the command. The drum major is facing the unit as it approaches. The execution signal for a box reverse is given at the predetermined time as the right foot strikes the ground. For a countermarch there is no signal of execution; the maneuver commences as the drum major enters the first rank.

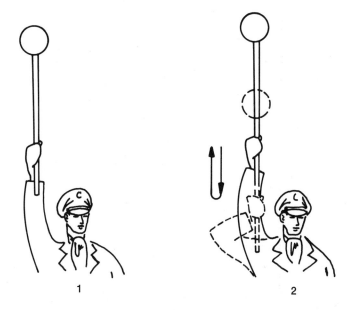

1   2

11. Close Width Interval. In order to have the unit close up the block formation widthwise, to parade on a narrow street, the drum major usually gives a baton signal but can, under some conditions, give the command verbally. The verbal command for the unit when it is moving without music is "Close interval—March." The command of execution, "March," comes as the left foot strikes the ground. When using the baton signal, the drum major raises both arms 45 degrees from the horizontal, forming an angle of about 90 degrees between them. The baton is in his right hand and is pointed out as an extension of his right arm. His back is to the organization. When he has held this pose long enough to attract the attention of the entire unit (about six seconds) he slowly brings both arms to a vertical position, for

Diagram 14 / **Close width interval** 1. Signal of preparation: This is the first phase of the command. Preparatory signal is as illustrated and should be held at least six seconds. 2. Signal of execution: This is the second phase of the command. The execution command is given as the left foot strikes the ground. The drum major must remember that the unit will emerge from this at the half step.

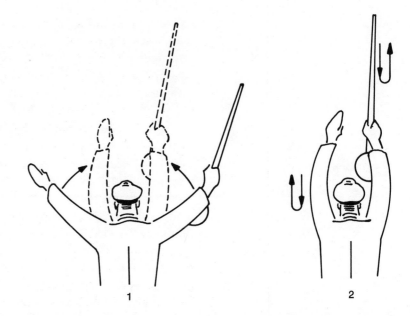

which no count is necessary. Then as a left foot strikes the ground he lowers both arms about a foot and then thrusts upward with both arms in a quick motion, down—up. The up motion should climax as the left foot hits the ground. The execution of the movement is begun on the next right foot. See *Diagram 14*.

12. Open Width Interval. In order to open the unit from close interval to open interval or the block formation, the usual command is a baton signal. In some cases it may be a verbal command. The verbal command is "Open interval—March." The command of execution, "March," comes as the left foot strikes the ground. The execution is begun on the next right foot. The baton signal to bring the unit to open interval from close interval is the reverse of the signal to close. The

Diagram 15 / **Open width interval** 1. Signal of preparation: This is the first phase of the command. The preparatory signal is as illustrated and should be held at least six seconds. 2. Signal of execution: This is the second phase of the command. The execution command is given as the left foot strikes the ground. The drum major has his back to the unit and must remember that the unit emerges from this at the half step.

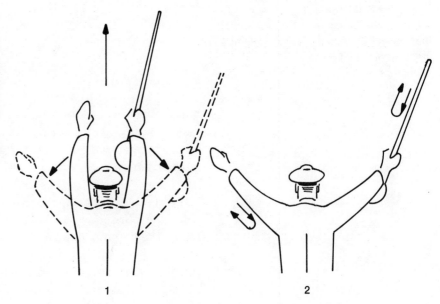

drum major, with his back to the unit, raises both arms directly over-head, pointing to the sky. When he has held this pose long enough to get the attention of his organization, he slowly spreads his arms side ways until he has formed a 90-degree angle between them. Then, as a left foot strikes the ground, both arms are drawn in toward the body, maintaining the 90-degree spread and thrust out on a quick down—up motion. The up thrust should climax as the left foot hits the ground. The execution of the maneuver is begun on the next right foot. See *Diagram 15.*

13. Maneuver or Formation Signal. In order to have simultaneous action on making or breaking a formation during a field show, the command can be a cue in the music or come from a baton signal. Since previous briefings and practices have designated the order and times of specific maneuvers, the baton signal to make and break any or all show formations can be limited to one. The drum major faces the organization with the tip of his baton pointing straight upward. At the appropriate time for the movement, the signal is given as the left foot strikes the ground. The baton is lowered about one foot, then jabbed straight up in a quick one—two count; one—down; two—up. See *Diagram 16.*

14. Alert signal. This is a signal to alert the unit that a standard baton signal is coming. It can be used in cases where it is necessary to be absolutely certain that the drum major gets undivided attention for a signal he is about to give. The only time it is really necessary with a well-trained unit is the instance in parades when the unit is approaching the reviewing stand and plans have been made to pass that stand with a special number, such as is described in Chapter 6 in the section titled "Competitions of Marching Musical Units." Of course, the alert signal can be used preceding any maneuver signal if so desired. It is not a preparatory or execution signal; it merely serves to alert the

Diagram 16 / **Maneuver or formation signal** 1. Signal of preparation: This is the first phase of the command. The signal is general and can be used to activate a predesignated maneuver or formation that is not cued to the music. Preparatory signal is as shown and should be held for six seconds. The unit should be ready for this signal anytime it is to be used, because of the program format. 2. Signal of execution: This is the second phase of the command. The drum major is facing the unit and at a predetermined point gives the signal of execution as illustrated. The execution signal is given on left foot.

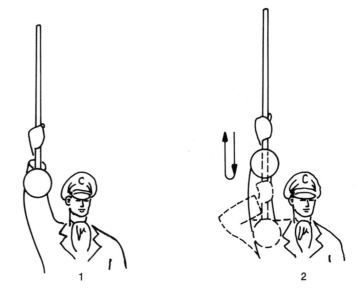

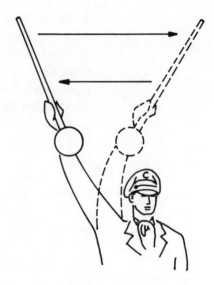

Diagram 17 / **Alert or caution** There is no first or second phase to this signal. It has no command of execution but nevertheless it is extremely important. It is of great value to alert the unit to the fact that it must be ready for the drum major's next signal, which may be one to counter something unexpected with which the unit has been confronted.

organization. Whether the drum major is facing or has his back toward the unit, whether he is moving or standing, he raises the baton high overhead, with the tip up, and waves it back and forth several times through a 90-degree arc to gain attention. See *Diagram 17*.

These baton signals are definite and few in number. They are easy for the drum major to master and easy for the men to understand. Having mastered them, the band can be paced through any problem with which it is confronted. Actually, there are only a few baton signals necessary to guide a band and these can be thought of in *groups*, such as the Halt Group, the Mark Time Group, the Open and Close Interval Group, the Start and Stop Music Group, etc. It is true that some of the signals have two or more meanings, such as the signal to start or stop the music. Here the same signal is used but no one could possibly interpret the signal to mean "stop the music" when the band

Diagram 18 / **Roll-off** This preparatory signal is recommended to directors who desire to use a standard roll-off to start playing while the band is in motion. The signal should be given at the beginning of a sixteen-measure drum cadence. This will give the drummers adequate time to prepare for the roll-off, which will be executed at the end of the cadence.

is not playing in the first place, nor could the signal mean "start the music" if the unit is already playing. See *Diagram 18*.

The importance of the drum major cannot be overemphasized since he is a key figure. Here are bits of advice for drum majors:

1. Remember that the entire organization depends upon you for guidance just as a football team depends on its quarterback. You must know your job from every possible angle and situation and be sure and exact, in order to hold the confidence of the unit.

2. You should endeavor to be the sharpest man in the unit; always alert, always an example in dress, actions, and so on.

3. You should know in detail all the set and improvised footwork and maneuvers and be able to explain and illustrate them.

4. You must know the music that will be played. This knowledge is necessary when cutting off the music or coordinating it with maneuvers. You should be present at all music rehearsals.

5. You should keep your baton signals to a minimum and work with the members in skull sessions and on the field until they know all your signals perfectly.

6. You should never use verbal commands if you can use your baton, since the baton is always used to convey commands under performance conditions.

7. You should not attempt to steal the show from the unit while guiding it. A certain amount of prancing looks good, but remember, you are there to guide the band.

8. You should think ahead so that you have readily available the best possible solution to any problem with which you or your unit might be confronted in a parade or on a field show. (If the organization overshoots a curve on a parade, is forced to half-step, or is crowded into the bleachers during a maneuver on a field show, it is definitely your fault.)

9. You should always make sure you have the attention of the entire organization when briefing the group or before giving a command of execution.

10. You should not use a whistle. A whistle is not necessary if you are good at your job.

11. You should not bring the organization to a half step at any time in a parade; this is an impossible step because lines, posture, in fact. everything, is destroyed. Use a full step until you bring the unit to mark time.

12. In a parade you should march at least twenty-five feet in front of the first rank of the unit. The distance you maintain in front of your unit designates your time cushion to solve an unexpected problem.

THE DRILL MASTER   The drill master can exert almost as much influence in creating a great marching musical unit as the director. He should be a nonplaying, nonmarching member of the unit and rank second in command to the director for all footwork, maneuvers, and military matters. He must have the whole-hearted support of the members, the director, and the subordinate leaders. His problems are greater and more numerous than those of any other member of the team except the director.

In selecting a person for this position it should be ascertained that he possesses qualifications similar to those cited for the drum major, plus some additional ones:

1. He should possess a working knowledge of fundamental and advanced footwork and formation design techniques in order to be able to train the musicians.

2. His voice should be strong. (A voice that demands respect and action.)

3. He should have had experience in the military service, and be sharp in dress and bearing.

4. He should be energetic and tenacious since the fruit of his effort does not come overnight.

The task of the drill master is to train the unit in precision footwork. His approach will determine whether or not his efforts will be successful. He must at all times be conscious of:

1. The personality factor. (See section at beginning of this chapter.)

2. Esprit de corps. (See section at end of this chapter.)

3. Formation and maneuver design. These must be worked out in detail as a constant process because, in this endeavor, extensive practice at designing is the only road to success.

4. The rewards of experimenting with designs. He should constantly experiment with designs of formations and maneuvers to make certain that he is using the best technique. (There is always a better way to execute a complicated task.)

5. The great value of assistants. He should very carefully select at least two qualified assistants to aid in formation planning. He should select an appropriate number of competent assistants to help him train the unit in footwork and maneuvers. (The drum major should be one of his assistants during the sectionalized footwork practices because the experience he gains working with a section will sharpen his techniques.)

This man who works behind the scenes is too important to place in a minor role. He is responsible for the visual appearance of the band, just as the director is responsible for the music, and yet when the unit performs he can at most be a spectator.

COMMANDS A command given either verbally or by baton is for the purpose of securing a coordinated response. Commands are usually divided into two phases:

a. The preparatory command informs the members of what is to be done. This phase requires no response whatsoever on the part of the unit members, except to consider the coming action. (Some bandsmen will change stride and disregard linework on the preparatory command in anticipation of the command of execution. This is incorrect and makes the organization appear untrained.)

b. The command of execution is an order to execute the preparatory command.

Examples of the preparatory command and the command of execution are: preparatory command—"Forward"; command of execution—"March." "Fall in," "At ease," and "Cover down" are a few examples of commands that do not require a separate preparatory or execution element.

At this point it is necessary to explain certain wording which has caused difficulty for new students reading texts on commands. Such phrases as "on the command of execution, execute a left flank," or "immediately on the command of execution, execute to the rear" may be poorly worded because it is impossible to execute a movement simultaneously with a command if one does not know exactly when the command will be given. *A movement is never executed on the command of execution but always on the next step or count.* For example, the command "March" of "Right flank—March," is voiced as the right foot strikes the ground, but the flank is executed by pivoting on the next foot, the left.

Perhaps a new term should be added to the command terminology. It could be called the time of execution and it is always one step or count following the command of execution, thus:

Preparatory Command	Command of Execution	Time of Execution
"Left flank—" (drawn out no count)	"March" (as a left foot strikes)	(as the following right foot strikes)

The fundamental concept that the correct execution of any order depends on the command cannot be diluted. Delivery is the all-important element. If the order is not seen or heard and understood by each and every person concerned, correct and coordinated response is impossible. Each and every order must be given in a manner that literally compels precise action on the part of every man in the unit. The qualities that inspire such responsive action are:

Voice Command	Baton Command
1. Snap	1. Visibility
2. Distinctness	2. Forcefulness
3. Power	3. Simplicity
4. Cadence	4. Cadence

Since baton tactics have already been covered in detail, the following discussion is limited to voice commands.

1. Snap

Snap is the professional quality in a voice command that obtains undivided attention. It expresses confidence and demonstrates complete understanding and control of the situation. The quality of snap is not a gift. Before a person can hope to attain this trait he must be certain of the mechanics of the action and must practice delivery. It is most utilized in commands of execution since it has been found that the elongated preparatory command is necessary to allow the unit members time for consideration. All of the elements of snap are brought into play in voicing a command of execution. The command should have the same effect, if properly delivered, as the starter's flag in an auto race.

Many factors contribute to snap in varying degrees:

    a. Complete understanding of the order.

    b. An erect military posture.

    c. Clear, distinct pronunciation.

    d. Controlled, but effortless breathing.

    e. Good resonance.

2. Distinctness

Distinctness in a command is necessary to secure coordinated action. A voice may have all other qualities but if it cannot be understood it will be ineffective. Distinctness depends upon proper use of the tongue, teeth, and lips in forming the correct sound. Many men have developed a very distinct voice quality by working with each command in a low voice, slowly increasing the volume as they correct the sound. Indistinct orders usually are the result of no training, poor training, or disinterest. In many cases, however, indistinctness is caused by nervousness, tight muscles in the tongue and throat, and uncertainty. Such commands usually sound garbled or slurred such as "F o o—u t—Hatch" for "Forward—March." Other commands for flank and column movements are even worse and the result is confusion. Commands must be distinct.

3. Power

Power is a quality that must be developed in varying degrees of intensity by every person who gives voice commands. Undue physical output or exertion is unnecessary and harmful. The vocal apparatus can be strained by tightening the throat muscles and freezing in general. This attitude may induce the person to believe that he is adding power to his voice, but the normal voice mechanisms are hampered and the result is a garbled, strained sound. To project the voice with power several factors must be understood:

    a. Good posture—this is self-evident.

    b. Proper breathing—try this experiment: Exhale all air from the lungs and attempt to yell "Hey." It cannot be done because of improper lung control.

    c. Correct use of the throat muscles and diaphragm: The most important muscle used in breathing is the diaphragm. This is the powerful muscle dividing the chest and abdominal cavities. It automatically controls the breathing unless forced to do otherwise. The diaphragm, specifically, plays a major role in giving commands because the muscle can force out powerful sounds. The diaphragm can be developed by deep breathing. The following exercise will demonstrate this idea:

The student should take a deep breath and, while holding the air in his lungs, open his mouth and relax all throat, jaw, and tongue muscles. He should enunciate "Ha" in as short a duration as possible. The sound should be made entirely by expelling short air puffs from the lungs, using only the muscles around the waist and the diaphragm. A distinct movement on the abdominal muscles will be felt. This process will develop power but requires extensive practice.

If so desired, further checks can be made into the voice aspect of effective commands. A speech teacher can be helpful by acquainting the student with other voice factors such as inflection, articulation, and resonance. All those who must give voice commands should develop a good voice quality within their own physical limitations.

4. Cadence

Cadence means a rhythm corresponding to the rhythm of the movement. It depends upon controlled breathing and proper voicing and, in addition, proper execution. The pause or interval between the preparatory and execution commands should be of a relatively uniform duration. It is a grave error on the part of a drill master to allow large variations in the length of the interval between the two commands because this keeps the unit members in a state of uncertainty.

The voice and its proper use are very effective tools of the trade for a director, drill master, drum major, and other key personnel who teach or command within a marching musical organization. One fine director understood the value of proper voice usage and enlisted the aid of the high school speech teacher. A two-hour lesson was given once a week to the unit's sixteen key personnel. In about one year the results were just short of phenomenal.

AN UPGRADE PROGRAM In order to utilize the "in-house" skills in each organization, avoid loss of time during rehearsals, maintain maximum interest on the part of the members, and increase the overall proficiency it is suggested that an upgrade program be formulated, adopted, and put into operation. An upgrade program is simple in structure and administration, but can be very productive.

First, the director, as the overall commander, should select a number of section leaders from the command line in the unit. (See section in this chapter on the chain of command.) These section leaders should be specialists in either footwork or music and should be considered staff assistants to the director. During sectional rehearsals or drills, they should straighten out the everyday-type problems within their sections, details which otherwise would require the director's time and attention.

Second, the director should call regular staff meetings. This will elevate the importance of the staff members, in both their own estimation and the eyes of the organization's members. He should assign projects to the staff and he will soon discover how staff assistants can be of immense value to his program.

It is also a great opportunity to train leaders and promote leadership. The structural pattern of marching bands and drum corps facilitates the implementation of an upgrade program. Most marching bands can be divided into three major sections:

1. Brass

2. Reeds

3. Percussion

The director should select a staff assistant for each major section. These assistants should be bandsmen who in his estimation have the highest qualities of musicianship and leadership. Next he must select section heads who in turn will be responsible for subsections:

1. Trumpet section

2. Clarinet section

3. Snare drum section

4. Etc.

Finally, he must select minor section heads to control the smallest groups that can be realistically broken out of the unit:

1. Second trumpet section

2. Second clarinet section

3. Etc.

All selections must be made with great care and on merit alone. (Beware of petty politics and partiality else the system will decay from within.)

The selection of staff assistants and the various section heads should not end with the musical requirements. The drill master should make his recommendations to the director for suitable assistants such as:

1. Field performance planners

2. Footwork specialists

3. Property custodians

Once the key personnel are appointed for both music and military matters, the director must indoctrinate them with his long-range plan for upgrading the unit. Some of the general factors he must stress are:

1. That a man in a key position has a responsibility, not only to the director and band at large, but also to each of his charges. No leader at any level can use his authority indiscriminately and be successful. (It is worthwhile to note that the most successful leaders use their authority in small and diplomatic quantities.)

2. That men in key positions make every effort to solve a problem themselves, before referring it to a higher authority.

3. That men in key positions have some leeway to use individual ideas and methods to legally accomplish the desired end product.

4. That the various subordinate leaders should not run "hot and cold." They must not overwork their sections for several weeks and then forget about the job for the next few. The best policy for continual improvement is a constant, light, and uniform pressure always in the desired direction.

5. That the realization of success in the entire endeavor will depend upon the different assistants carrying out the policy and assignments of the director and drill master.

After the selection of the men and the discussion on policy, procedures, and desired results, the actual mechanics of the operation must be considered. For example:

1. How often to practice as sections.

2. How long to practice at a sectional rehearsal.

3. What material should be covered.

4. Where should the sectional practices be held.

All of these questions can be answered only as they fit the needs of a particular unit. The director must build his program to match the needs and conditions of his organization. The following upgrade program was conducted by a very successful high school band director and a director of a championship drum corps in an adjacent community:

1. Minor section leaders met with their charges every other week for a maximum of two hours for music rehearsal. The meetings took place in the homes of the men in the minor sections. The evening on which the men met was determined by majority rule in each minor section. (It might be well to note here both directors stated that the families of the men concerned came to be avid supporters of the units. The process grew into families meeting families, until the units had the benefits not only of the practices, but also of the solid family support.)

2. Major and subsection leaders met with their respective groups once every other week for a maximum of two hours in the unit's regular rehearsal hall and split the time as required.

3. The director gave the various section leaders a good idea of what he desired and left the rest to them.

4. Both units, also, had one sectional practice outside on footwork and maneuvers each week. This was limited to two hours and was conducted with and without instruments.

5. In each of these two cases, the directors merely spot-checked the operations and confined their activities to full rehearsals and planning.

Many band leaders attempt to build a good unit by doing everything alone. By constantly driving themselves, they attain various degrees of success. Actually their success could be much greater if the responsibilities of the job were disseminated among the top personnel of the organization. The director should act in the capacity of leader and advisor to his assistants. The best drummer, for example, can rehearse the percussion section. To him, the percussion section is the most important part of the band, whereas to the director it is just one section. This applies equally to the sax section, brass section, soprano bugle section, and so on. The director can rehearse one section at a time, but with section leaders directing their particular groups, the entire band can be working at one time in different locations. The abilities of the top men should never be underestimated. They will prove themselves invaluable in relieving the leader of tasks they can perform most efficiently.

This program can be very constructive and will, in a period of a few years, create a great band. Quality will be self-generating in the marching band when fueled by a spirit of competition.

Finally, a word of caution concerning the implementation of an upgrade program. It is built slowly and gains strength as it goes. It should take a minimum of six months to put the system in functioning order, but if kept up, it pays off ever afterward.

ESPRIT DE CORPS Every person who has ever had command of a group has been confronted with a will-of-the-wisp intangible factor called esprit de corps. Its twin, morale, is heard of more frequently and sometimes these two words are used interchangeably. There is a difference between the terms morale and esprit de corps. Morale is basically an individual feeling concerning a man's outlook and attitude toward his daily life. Esprit de corps is a common feeling or attitude of a group, and it is an attitude that does not change as quickly or as frequently as morale.

Many writers have attempted to define esprit de corps; their definitions vary considerably. It is a qualitative rather than a quantitative term, and a distinct definition is difficult but we do know that certain things are necessary and others must be avoided in order to create esprit de corps. Consider the following points:

1. Technical proficiency. The leaders must be able to demonstrate that they are well schooled in their technical specialties, whether it be music, footwork, formations, or administrative factors. If a man wants a job done and doesn't know the techniques, he will not be able to inspire his charges. Here a word of moderation is necessary. It is not intended that the director, who must concern himself with the music, administration, and policy making, should also design formations and personally conduct close-order drill. However, he should have a working knowledge of these factors and show his technical proficiency in music matters.

2. Personal interest. The names of the members in the organization should be memorized and used. If a problem arises, the director or the appropriate section head should always be ready to help.

3. A definite program. The leader should always be able to outline a definite program for any practice, performance, or event. If he does not know exactly what he wishes done, the organization certainly cannot respond in a definite manner.

4. Coordination. As soon as the leader learns of anything that will affect the unit he should inform the members. If he does not trust the

members on matters that concern them, they will not have confidence in him. He should always remember that they may be able to offer a better solution to a problem than the one pending.

5. Critique. After every practice or performance, a critique should be held where constructive criticism can be offered.

6. Impartiality. The leader should never set apart a few members of the unit as special pets. The others will resent this and probably form cliques of their own. The only clique that can be condoned is the one in which every member of the unit is a participant.

7. Prima donnas. Nothing demoralizes an organization more than to have one or two members collect all the praise for themselves and try to hold center stage. It must be impressed upon the members that they are a team.

8. Discipline. No group can work together without discipline. It is not necessary to use a whip to be a disciplinarian. A constant movement in the right direction is required. It is a great mistake to run hot and cold, severe one day or week, and lax the next. The perfect formula is a gentle, constant pressure. Work on small matters of discipline as they appear and large problems in discipline will be rare.

9. Personal projects. One way a leader can convince the members of an organization that he is backing them is always to have a personal project under way. This project must be something that is difficult for the members to accomplish, but at the same time it must be a project that will benefit the organization. The project might be a campaign to raise money for a tape recorder, movie equipment or a trip. Continuity is essential—as soon as one project is accomplished, the director should have another at hand.

10. A goal. A goal must always be set toward which the entire organization will work. As the unit nears the goal it should be moved still higher. No one ever reaches a state of absolute perfection; therefore, the goal can always be pushed nearer to the perfection stage.

11. Interest by internal competition. A healthy competitive spirit within the organization itself is a great asset and will add to the overall interest. It is not too difficult to set up a system of competition. Each year a certificate can be awarded to the best drummer, the best trombone man, the best military man, the best rookie member, and so on. Certificates are cheap, but the benefits that can be derived from them cannot be measured. This competitive spirit can boomerang if the competition is not based strictly on merit.

12. Order and cleanliness. The condition of the rehearsal areas and supply rooms has a great effect on the attitude of the members. If these are orderly and clean, the right attitude is established. If the areas are not clean, and there is no orderly system for storage, seating, etc., it will infect the members.

13. Seniority. Through trial and error many leaders have found that seniority is not always a good guiding rule. If a position of rank in the organization is to be filled, and there are two men available who could fill it equally well as regards proficiency, worth, and interest, then it should go to the man with the seniority. If one man has two years'

seniority and the other four years', yet the newer man is much better qualified, more attentive, and more cooperative, then the newer man should be selected. The other member may feel slighted, but the unit will realize that the general welfare is all-important.

14. Inspections. Each time the unit has a full-dress performance, it should be assembled five to fifteen minutes early to permit a spot check on the condition of uniforms, shoes, instruments, etc. This inspection before each and every performance will sharpen the unit's appearance, and in a short time the personnel will be checking each other before the inspection. It should be a formal ritual. The drum major should assemble the unit in block formation, covered down. The inspection should be run from the front to the back rank in the following manner: The drum major calls the unit to attention and then gives all except the A rank parade rest. The inspector can walk along the front of the rank, then check the back by walking between ranks A and B. Once he has inspected the front and back of the A rank, the drum major should call the B rank to attention and give the A rank parade rest. This sequence is continued until the entire unit has been inspected. This inspection can be done at a slow walk; there is no need for the inspector to stop unless a discrepancy is noticed. The inspection should be made only by the director, drill master, or drum major.

Esprit de corps is not built in a week or a month. It requires a long time and cannot be acquired unless an organization has been through the lowest ebbs and emerged battle-marked, but intact. Esprit de corps is the ghost factor that will point to one organization as being greater than another, although both of them may be of equal technical proficiency.

It is even an egotistical air that members carry in their hearts, feeling that they belong to the finest, and then are willing to prove it to themselves by trying even harder. And so one can go on with statements that are not concrete, but all aimed in the general direction of this shadowy and elusive ingredient—esprit de corps.

**TIPS ON FORMATION /
MANEUVER DESIGN AND
REHEARSAL**

The total design and rehearsal time for a single maneuver can easily pass the 1,000-man-hour mark and therefore is a matter of deep concern to the director as well as to key personnel. The route to be followed in producing a good maneuver or formation showpiece is complex. There are methods, pitfalls, detours, and shortcuts in each design effort. There are also certain limitations to design work, and there are instances where minor changes will almost double the precision and audience appeal. It is important that the responsible personnel be aware of all such possibilities. Although the design work and formation rehearsals are separately identifiable entities, they are inseparably interwoven. Here, as in all arts and crafts, there are rules and tricks of the trade:

1. Tips on Design Efforts
   a. Design personnel
      The director should have a design team composed of the drill master and several assistants. While it is not impossible to have one active, interested designer do all the formation and maneuver work, it is not a good practice. There are too many shortcomings that can cause problems. For example:
      (1) The single designer may lose close contact with his organization due to the time involved in creating designs.
      (2) The design effort can become stereotyped.
      (3) The design work depends upon the constant availability of the one designer.
      (4) A design team can pinpoint errors more readily than an individual.
   b. Tools of the designer
      Some tools are necessary to design formations. Several of the more common ones are miniature football fields with figures depicting the bandsmen; blackboards which facilitate easy changes; drafting instruments to make exotic overlay sets which are fine for illustrating a design sequence. Tools that are always available are paper, pencil, and ruler. Any formation can be designed completely on a large sheet of paper, and 95 percent of all field problems can be solved in the same manner.
   c. Design sequence

When planning a formation/maneuver design, the following sequence is recommended:

(1) Establish a firm idea of what is desired.
(2) Draw sketches of the various ideas on the block formation dot sheets.
(3) Prepare finished drawings of the accepted designs.
(4) Mimeograph copies of the completed work for handouts.
(5) Schedule skull sessions.

d. Standardized performance area

Standardization of the performance area is of the utmost importance as it assists the design team. An entire football field is ideal as a standard. The dimensions are perfect as they afford maneuvering space, and then, too, such fields are common items. The performance area should not be interpreted as an area over which one formation or maneuver is spread. It should signify the space within which all the formations/maneuvers and activities will take place, i.e., entrance, formations, maneuvers, and departure. Once a standard area has been selected, all personnel associated with the organization will have the same concept in mind when planning or discussing designs and rehearsals.

e. Types of design

There are three general types of formations and maneuvers:

(1) The explosive type. Here all bandsmen proceed to designated points by the most direct route and in the quickest possible time. General confusion is the theme while the unit members enter or leave a formation.
(2) The precision type. Here definite routes are used for marching. A picture unfolds and refolds before the eyes of the public, and all is orderly and precise. The audience will be able to deduce what the picture will be before it is completely formed and usually enjoys guessing correctly.
(3) Script writing. Here a continuous line of bandsmen play "follow the leader."

f. Significance of design

Every design should have some significance so as to draw the audience into the show. As an example, it is not appropriate to form a football for a Memorial Day salute.

g. Stationary positions

Designs that permit a number of men to hold fast and serve as guides assist in the execution of the formation and result in greater precision. The design ideas should be superimposed on the block formation dot sheets and adjusted to retain as many guide men as possible (see the pilot's wings formation).

h. Reform the block after each formation

The design should decree the block be reformed following each single show formation or maneuver.

(1) Maneuvering from and back to the block requires no more effort or rehearsal time than going from one formation to

another. Actually it requires less rehearsal time. Once the return to the block becomes SOP, every member of the unit will know what to expect and will respond accordingly. Everyone will soon realize that the routes taken to return to the block are always opposite to the routes taken to go into a formation. There are many advantages to reforming the block after each formation.

(a) It always adds movement to the show.

(b) It makes it possible to use any formation or maneuver within a show as a portion of another show without redesigning the work or adding additional rehearsal time.

(c) The return to the block is the key to a fine library of formations and the economical use of man-hours.

(d) The block provides a standard starting point for each formation and in this way eliminates any confusion in the minds of the members. It also serves as a recovery point for any member who may inadvertently become confused while in formation.

(2) Since it is usually possible to go from the block into a formation and return to the block with fewer than sixty-four bars of music, little or no time is lost. There is the added advantage of almost constant motion, making the formation appear more complicated than it actually is. Movement is a key to a successful marching unit show. The more coordinated movement that can be put into a maneuver or formation, the better the spectacle.

i. The advantage of action

Remember, the audience is interested primarily in seeing a spectacle; therefore, a maximum amount of movement should always be designed into formation and maneuver work. Well-planned and coordinated movement in the proper amount creates much of the spectacle. Units that go into a formation and spend the allotted time saluting an audience, from one design, do not live up to their charter because by definition they are *marching* musical units.

It is possible to design good animation into all formation work. Additional movements can frequently be added. When the unit moves into a formation a coordinated facing should be made. This should be timed with some phrase in the music, instead of having each man face the audience separately. Following the coordinated facing, several mark-time steps and an exaggerated halt can be effectively used. Such coordinated facings and halts can be used for all formations, and every time the block is reformed. Should the facing and halt techniques just described be used, they should be employed at all times so that they become a ritual, engrained in the minds of the bandsmen. If the techniques are used only periodically they will create confusion. When a field show is designed, it should be composed to ascertain maximum animation. As a general rule it is unwise to remain in a fixed position for more than one minute.

j. Spontaneous action

When many units break a formation, some personnel are sure to move several steps late. This problem can be overcome, and at the same time excellent formation breaks achieved, by instructing the members that in *all* instances, following the signal or cue to break, two mark-time steps should be executed in place, before the break is made. This will give a spontaneous and coordinated formation break since the mark-time steps act as a warning. Since those who break a formation late are usually different members on different occasions, this method will do much to correct the problem. This trick of beginning a formation break by first marking time two steps and then stepping off must be used consistently or it will merely add another element of confusion.

k. Visual balance

Formations and maneuvers should have symmetry if maximum appeal and sharpness are desired. Each part and counterpart should be identical. As an example, if a set of "pilot's wings" is formed and a tuba is stationed at the left wing tip, there should also be a tuba on the right wing tip. This visual symmetry can become a complicated problem at times when the designers are attempting to keep instrumental voicing together, but experience gained through trial and error will make each confrontation easier than the last.

l. Musical balance

In designing a formation, musical balance must be considered. It is especially important to keep the percussion section in the center of formations. In the pilot's wings formation, shown later in this chapter, the percussion instruments should be in the shield, not placed on the wing tips. The percussion section is the "heartbeat" of the unit. Never divide it. To do so can lead to disaster. A solid beat from a central location will keep the unit together and give the director complete control.

m. Music to fit the formation

In order to obtain the best results in designing a formation, design it without regard for the music. The music can always be made to fit the pattern, but the reverse is extremely difficult. This concept is illustrated by matching the music by a design sequence for a single show formation. The procedure is as follows:

(1) Design the show formation.

(2) Establish the formation positions.

(3) Determine the routings to the formation positions (maximum number of steps into formation for this example is twenty-eight).

     (4) *Now* fit the music to the formation as follows:

       (a) Mark time two steps at the start of the music, break the block, and proceed into formation.

       (b) Make coordinated facings to the audience on the thirty-first and thirty-second beats, since the thirty-second beat is a phrase ending.

       (c) Halt the mark time with a baton cue from the drum major.

       (d) Play music desired from the show formation position.

       (e) Break the show formation and proceed back into the block formation on the ninety-seventh beat or immediately after any phrase ending.

       (f) Make coordinated facings to the audience on the last two beats of a music phrase.

       (g) Halt the mark time with a baton cue and step off immediately into the next formation or upon the drum major's cue. (Fitting the music to the design sequence is not difficult. After a little practice a designer/musician team can become quite expert at it.)

n. Spotlight the band

Whenever the band is doing a production number, feature the band. Do not distract the attention of the audience by spotlighting a mascot, baton twirler, trick rope artist, etc. Such features can be worked into the performance at appropriate places, but they should not compete for attention at the expense of the entire organization.

2. Tips on Rehearsal

  a. Orientation for the drum major

For each new show, even on the home arena, the drum major and drill master should pace off all distances on the actual area to be used. While he is doing this, he can mentally visualize the performance that will take place. While this may sound like a small item, it accomplishes two purposes. First, embarrassing errors may be prevented; and second, the *exact* starting position can be set and formation positions centered. (In some field shows it is necessary to start off-center in order to center the bulk of the show. The drum major should determine exactly where he must position the pacesetter to begin all shows.)

  b. Cues from the drum major

Excessive use of the baton should be avoided. The drum major can alert the members of an approaching music cue without the use of his baton. For example, during the show formation the drum major is usually facing the audience. Just prior to the musical cue to break the formation, he can execute an about-face and stand at attention facing the band. This is a small tactic that can be used to inform the unit members of the approaching change.

c. Orientation for the unit

The time schedule should allow the members an opportunity to observe the performance area. If they can do this they will be less apt to be distracted when they begin the show.

d. Tuning instruments

The oldest and best suggestion for tuning and giving final instructions to marching musical organizations is to select a spot removed from the audience. Should the unit be taken to a point from which the members will have visual access to the performance area after the tuning no ad lib solo should be permitted. Traits all champions possess are assurance and poise. Both traits can be destroyed by noisy toots and drum taps which indicate poor training, lack of discipline, and nervousness.

The preceding suggestions taken individually may be rated as minor factors but used collectively they will give a great advantage to the organization.

FORMATION DESIGN PROCEDURES AND TECHNIQUES —THE PILOT'S WINGS

Designing a complete formation or maneuver for a marching musical unit is not easy. In an attempt to assist the designer we shall show detailed procedures for several designs. *Remember, these formations are not illustrated for your marching unit. They are placed in this book to detail procedures and techniques to assist design teams on certain types of design work!*

The pilot's wings formation

Let's start with the problem of designing a formation to salute the Air Force. Utilize a unit of sixty members with an established interval of sixty inches.

1. The process of considering different design ideas is handled much better by a design team than by one person. The discussion often results in a fine idea, one that was not even listed to be discussed. The design selection process is important and should be used previous to actual design work. In this example, the pilot's wings were chosen as the best idea for a salute. Other suggestions were considered and discarded. The reasoning went as follows:

a. On the negative side:

(1) It would be impossible to form any type of airplane on the field that would appear realistic.

(2) Should the letters USAF be used, more manpower than the sixty-man marching unit would be required to form a good solid picture.

(3) A propeller can be too easily mistaken for something else.

b. On the positive side:

(1) The pilot's wings make a very good picture in two dimensions.

(2) They are very representative of the Air Force and its mission.

(3) They have no feature that might be misinterpreted by any person or group.

2. After determining the formation that will be used for a particular purpose, the task of designing the formation follows. This requires several reference diagrams depicting the unit concerned. These diagrams should be drawn on standard size paper which can easily be reproduced. A reference diagram showing the alphabetical and numerical nomenclature of all positions in the unit is absolutely necessary. This sheet is shown as *Diagram 19*, labeled Position Chart. Another reference

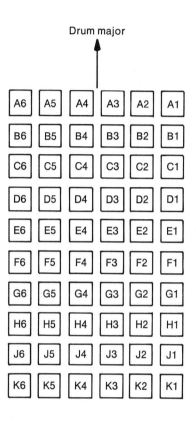

Diagram 19 / **Position chart** Note: A, B, C, etc., are ranks; 1. 2, 3, etc., are files.

diagram shows the instrumentation of the entire unit in block formation. This sheet assists the design team during the construction of the formation. Two instrumentation sheets are shown: one for a band, *Diagram 20a*, and another for a drum and bugle corps, *Diagram 20b*. A third type of reference sheet (*Diagram 21*) shows the block formation represented by dots. This is the basic sheet on which possible formations are sketched in (see *Diagram 22*). Since a great many sketch sheets may be used in creating one design, an adequate supply should be available.

With the idea established and the reference sheets available, the formation design progresses to the next step, which is making trial sketches to determine the exact picture to be formed by the unit. This is the first attempt that is made to put the formation on paper. The beginning of the sketching endeavor should be as elementary as possible. The designer, using these sheets, sketches various possibilities until he arrives at the one most satisfactory. Fifty may be necessary. The sketching is easily and quickly done, and by making a series of

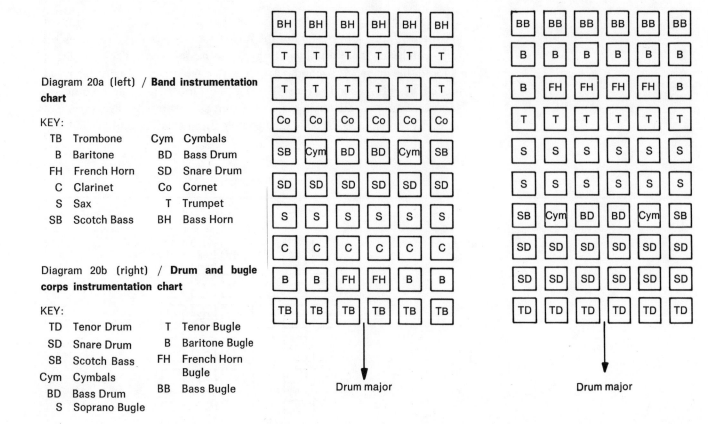

Diagram 20a (left) / **Band instrumentation chart**

KEY:

TB	Trombone	Cym	Cymbals
B	Baritone	BD	Bass Drum
FH	French Horn	SD	Snare Drum
C	Clarinet	Co	Cornet
S	Sax	T	Trumpet
SB	Scotch Bass	BH	Bass Horn

Diagram 20b (right) / **Drum and bugle corps instrumentation chart**

KEY:

TD	Tenor Drum	T	Tenor Bugle
SD	Snare Drum	B	Baritone Bugle
SB	Scotch Bass	FH	French Horn Bugle
Cym	Cymbals		
BD	Bass Drum	BB	Bass Bugle
S	Soprano Bugle		

Drum major

Drum major

drawings, many ideas previously unthought of will come to the designer. Our elementary concept decrees that the block formation should always be visualized as the very heart of the design and the expansions must be made from this center or focus. The use of the sketch sheet with two sketches is shown in *Diagram 22*, entitled Sketch sheet.

Diagram 21 / **Block formation dot sheet** 1. This sketch sheet shows the long axis of the unit aligned with the long axis of the paper. 2. Other sketch sheets with the long axis of the unit aligned with the short axis of the paper should be available. 3 An ample supply of both types of sketch sheets should be available before starting any design. 4. The following scales of dot sheets are recommended: a. one established interval = ¼ inch. b. one established interval = ½ inch. c. one established interval = 1 inch.

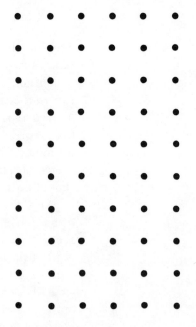

3. When the sketches have been made and one selected, it then becomes the task of the designer to determine the routings and the positions the bandsmen must use for the execution of the formation. This is the most tedious and exacting task confronting the designer. For this work the use of the dotted reference sheet is indispensable. There are many routes that can be used to enter any formation, but one routing scheme can always be found that is superior to the others. After the necessary routing and positioning diagrams are completed they can be placed on standard sized sheets and copies of them distributed to each member. The bandsman can then study his formation

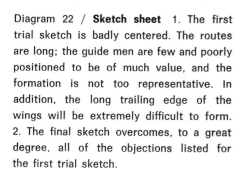

Diagram 22 / **Sketch sheet** 1. The first trial sketch is badly centered. The routes are long; the guide men are few and poorly positioned to be of much value, and the formation is not too representative. In addition, the long trailing edge of the wings will be extremely difficult to form. 2. The final sketch overcomes, to a great degree, all of the objections listed for the first trial sketch.

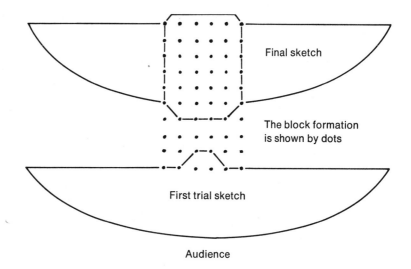

Final sketch

The block formation is shown by dots

First trial sketch

Audience

position and the route that must be taken to get into that position. See *Diagrams 23 and 24.* One more item is necessary to make the design data complete. That item is the written explanation of the footwork.

4. Explanation of footwork in the pilot's wings formation as per diagram:

 a. General notes:

  (1) The wing formation must be started from an exact block formation.

  (2) The scale of the diagram is determined by the scale of the sketch sheet. It is wise to have several different sketch sheet sizes or scales.

 b. On the command of execution, either by baton or musical cue, two mark-time steps are made, then the following action takes place:

  (1) K1 steps off at a right angle to the number one file, takes twenty established paces, and then marks time. It is very important that K1 steps out at a right angle and marches in a straight line, since he establishes the track for the left leading edge of the wings.

  (2) K2 and K3 step off to the right and follow K1 at established intervals.

  (3) The entire number three file, with the exception of K3, executes to the rear and steps off in file. Each in turn, except D3, upon

Diagram 23 / **Routing diagram**

KEY:

● Block position

◉ Formation position

▣ Formation position of guide men

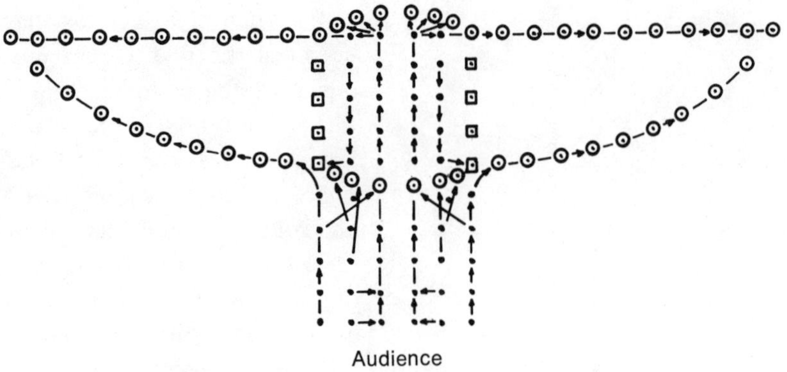

Audience

reaching the block position or original position of K3, must execute a left flank and follow, at sixty-inch intervals, the route taken by K1, K2, and K3. When D3 reaches the block position of K3 he takes one additional full pace forward and marks time. This leaves one double interval between E3 and C3, but this is closed by C3 when E3 reaches his formation position.

(4) A2 steps off to the left and executes a left flank two paces later, upon reaching the block position of A3. A2 then follows A3 until he reaches the block position of K3, at which time he goes into position, as illustrated by the routing diagram.

(5) B2 faces left and must mark time four steps until A2 is passing the block position of B3. He then takes two paces and executes a left flank on the block position of B3 and follows A2 until he reaches the block position of K3. At this point he goes into his formation position as shown by the routing diagram.

(6) G1, H1, and J1 do not move from their block positions, but on the command of execution they mark time in place. These are key men or guide men.

(7) Although F1 moves in the process of forming the wings, he moves so little that he can be termed a key position man. At the command of execution F1 takes two fifteen-inch steps backward and marks time until the last man in the trailing edge passes him. At this time he takes a full pace forward into his block formation position, which is also his wings formation position.

Diagram 24 / **Formation position designation**

KEY:

◉ Wing formation position

▣ Wing formation position of guide men

Audience

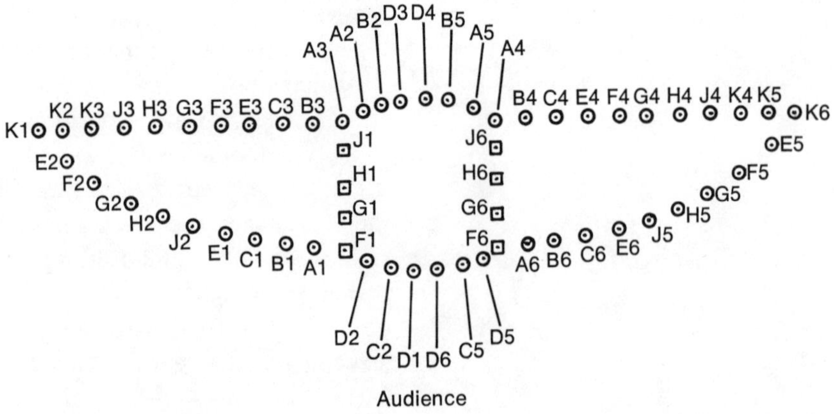

(8) E2 executes to the rear and, following the route indicated in the diagram, passes over the block formation position of F1. E2 then establishes his route to determine the curvature of the left trailing edge of the wings. This is the most difficult part of the entire formation because when E2 begins to establish his curve, K1, who is establishing the left leading edge of the wings, is not yet in place. Therefore, E2 is creating the curve on an open field. K1 should arrive in his final position about six paces ahead of E2. The curve created by E2 must be as indicated in the diagram. As E2 passes the block position of F1, he is followed by F2, G2, H2, and J2, in that order, according to the route illustrated. As J2 passes the block formation position of F1 he is followed by E1, C1, B1, and A1, as shown. When A1 has reached his position in the wings, F1 takes one step forward into his wings formation position.

(9) D1 turns left, as the diagram indicates, and steps forward into the open space between files one and two, where he marks time until all the men have cleared his route. D1, C2, and D2 then go into position as shown in the diagram.

The entire left half of the pilot's wings is now formed. The right half is formed at the same time. It is easy to see that the formation is symmetrical and that each half is developed at exactly the same time and in the same manner, with the exception of the direction of turns. (It is not considered necessary to give a detailed written description of the development of the right half of the formation.)

5. At this point, picture the bandsmen in the wings formation, all facing in various directions marking time and playing. The question of how to face the audience now arises. There are several ways in which this can be effected. Four follow:

a. Each man, upon reaching his wings position, can turn to face the audience and continue to mark time until the drum major halts the group. (This is the easiest method, but not the best.)

b. Each man can halt on a musical cue, then "in cadence" face the audience. (This method is an improvement over a. above.)

c. The turn can be made on a musical cue and the mark time continued until halted on a musical cue or by the drum major.

d. The men can turn on the right foot to face the audience at a predetermined point in the music. The halt is made by throwing out the left foot during the turn and then setting it smartly beside the right at its completion. This is a difficult maneuver. This flashy turn and halt require practice, but it is certainly worth the time and effort spent in perfecting it. It is accomplished in a one—two count; turn on "one" and halt on "two." Keep in mind that this one—two turn and halt can be used on many occasions with different formation work and routine practice work.

6. The wing formation can be broken on either a musical cue or a signal from the drum major. The men return to the block formation by reversing their route of entry. As each man reaches his position, he faces the audience and covers while marking time. When the block is reformed and all members are marking time, the unit can either halt and then step off on cue, or step off on a signal into its next formation.

If the unit is well trained on the mark time and halt, it will add greatly to the value of the formation.

7. Notes on the wing formation:

a. Since the spacing in the formation must be exact it should be started from an aligned block formation. Should the block be disoriented in spacing and coverage, the wing formation will have less chance of being aligned.

b. The formation takes advantage of using men who do not move to serve as guides.

c. The formation, in the process of being created, becomes a fine animated spectacle.

d. Actually, only four men have difficult jobs in the formation. They are K1 and K6, who generate the leading edges of the wings, and E2 and E5, who generate the trailing edges of the wings. These men should be instructed not to play while marching to their positions. They should concentrate on their marching. Once they are in position they can resume playing.

e. Notice the formation locations of D1 and D6. These two members appear to take an awkward route to these positions, but there is a good reason. Note the drum and bugle corps instrumentation diagram on which this design was based. D1 and D6 are scotch bass drums, and these two instruments were so positioned to display coordinated stick work and to create visual balance. Note also that D3 and D4, the bass drummers, are placed side by side; thus, the heart of the rhythm section is in the center of the formation—a very important consideration.

The pilot's wings formation has now been covered in detail. It is a fine, showy, well-balanced, and significant maneuver. The design techniques depicted here can be applied directly to all precision-type formations. A novice in designing formations or a reader who has never worked on formation designs may find the task somewhat difficult for the initial learning period. The work becomes easier and more enjoyable with each new challenge.

THE LETTER M The identical design process used to develop the pilot's wings formation is used to develop the letter M formation. The letter M is one of the ten letters of the alphabet that will permit a symmetrical formation; however, letters, even symmetrical ones, should be used infrequently in field performances. See *Diagram 25.*

1. General notes

a. The formation is designed for a sixty-piece marching unit whose established pace is thirty inches.

b. The sequence for the letter M originates and ends in the block.

c. The audience is faced by the musicians in a different manner than those so far described to illustrate that the designers have options on just about every item of a formation or maneuver.

d. The entire picture with the routings shown looks complicated, but the footwork required of each member is quite simple. No

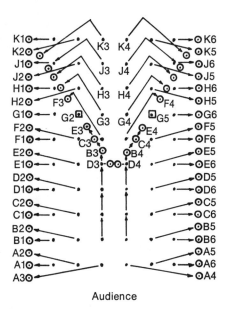

Diagram 25 / **Formation design: The letter M**

KEY:

● Block position

⊙ Formation position

▣ Formation position of guide men

Audience

member should be required to do complicated footwork for any formation with the limited significance of the letter M.

2. Footwork

a. On the command of execution two mark-time steps are taken by the entire unit.

b. All members of file one, A1 through K1, then execute four fifteen-inch right side steps and then mark time until the coordinated halt is made. Note that the first step of file one is a right side step, even through the music indicates a step on the left foot. File one can make the first (left) mark-time step in place and then continue with the four right side steps.

c. All members of file six, A6 through K6, execute four left fifteen-inch side steps and then mark time until the coordinated halt is made.

d. File two, A2 through K2, with the exception of G2, lifts the left foot as in mark time and simultaneously turns 90 degrees right on the ball of the right foot. The left foot is then set down beside the right in a mark-time step. All of this is executed in one count. The mark time, including the 90-degree right turn, totals four steps. On the fifth count, A2 through K2, with the exception of G2, step off into the intervals in file one, as indicated. The number two men should march into their positions in file one by guiding right. Once the number two men are in file one, they turn left to face the audience and continue to mark time. G2 holds fast and marks time.

e. File five, A5 through K5, with the exception of G5, lifts the left foot as in mark time and turns 90 degrees left on the ball of the right foot. The left foot is set down beside the right in a mark-time step. (This is executed in one count.) The mark time, including the 90-degree left turn, totals four steps. On the fifth count, A5 through K5, with the exception of G5, step off into the intervals in file six as indicated. Once the number five men are in file six, they turn right to face the audience. G5 holds fast and marks time.

f. G2 and G5 are guide men in that they have the same positions both in the block and in the M formation. They merely mark time during the construction of the M.

g. A3 faces 80 degrees right and proceeds into position as shown in the diagram. A4 faces 80 degrees left and does likewise.

h. B3, C3, D3, and E3 execute to the rear. E3 takes one pace to the rear of his block position, executes an improvised left oblique, and marches to within one established pace of G2. D3 marches two paces to the rear of his block position and executes an improvised right flank. D3 must clear the route to allow C3 and B3 to go into their M formation positions. D4 must do the same for C4 and B4. If D3 and D4 are bass drummers and if they flanked right and left respectively, toward each other, they could not advance enough, because of the bass drums, to clear the routes just mentioned. This situation can be handled in various manners:

(1) D3 executes an improvised right flank on the block position of E3. He pivots 90 degrees right again on the ball of the left foot (this makes him face the audience), then he takes one left side step and he is in position. D4 uses the same procedure with the exception of the turn and side step direction.

(2) D3 takes one left side step from his block position, and D4 takes one right side step from his block position, then both of them take four one-half established paces backward. This is very simple and it puts them in their M formation position facing the audience. This clears the route for the passage of C3, B3, C4, and B4. (Little difficulties such as route conflicts and blockages should always be worked out on the drawing board—not on the field!)

i. C3 marches one step beyond the block position of E3, executes an improvised left oblique, and marches to within one established pace of E3. B3 marches one step beyond the block position of E3 and executes an improvised left oblique. This will place B3 within one pace of C3. When B3, C3, and E3 are in the M position described, they turn left 150 degrees to face the audience.

j. B4, C4, D4, and E4 execute their movements as described in h. (above) with the exception of the direction of the flank and the obliques.

k. F3, G3, H3, J3, and K3 execute to the rear, but on the step-off they bear 30 degrees left. F3 marches on the route designated, one pace beyond G2, and turns left as indicated. The routes and turns for G3, H3, J3, and K3 are indicated and, after a skull session, one walk-through on the practice field will orient the marching musicians as to the required procedure.

l. F4, G4, H4, J4, and K4 execute as described in k. (above) with the exception of the direction of turn.

m. At this point every member is in his M formation position facing the audience and marking time.

3. Notes on the M formation

a. All members face the open end of the M (the audience and drum major) as soon as they are in their M positions.

b. With the letter M completely formed, all members are facing the audience and marking time; the mark time can be halted on a musical cue or a signal from the drum major. If the music for the M is short the men can mark time and end the mark time with an exaggerated halt at the end of the music.

c. For the purpose of instrument clearance and a clear view of the drum major, it may be desirable to have all the men in the two legs of the M face about 45 degrees toward the inside of the M. This is acceptable if the alignment is not distorted.

d. There are only two guide men, G2 and G5, in the M. These are at the strategic points of the V segment of the M. The legs are easy to form since the right and left flank men take only four side steps.

e. When file one moves four right side steps, the men usually remain covered adequately. When file two turns and feeds into the intervals in file one, the alignment may become distorted. This is caused by the number one men attempting to cover on the number two men. File one tends to forget that it was in position before the number two men entered. This can be overcome by stressing that the number one men hold their exact alignment (marking time) when the number two men enter the intervals in the number one file. The number two men must align themselves with the number one men who were in position first.

f. The block is reformed in the reverse manner.

g. Notice should be taken that the maximum number of steps into the M formation, by any one man, is eight. There are the initial two mark-time steps, plus six mark-time steps for alignment once in formation. Only sixteen beats are necessary for the entire process, which means the M is formed in about eight seconds.

Notes on letter designs   The pros and cons of using letters of the alphabet or numbers as part of a field show are important considerations. Many marching musical units consistently use letters and/or numbers as the major portion of their field show. Such formations merit a few comments:

1. A letter or number is as difficult, and in many cases more difficult, to design and execute than a figure of an anchor, music lyre, cross, rocket, face, or other pictorial illustration.

2. A letter or number formation in a field show is rather uninteresting to an audience. A great marching unit having precision footwork and alignment can offset much of this, but even in such cases a pictorial design is far more interesting and effective than a letter or number design.

3. In the planning stages, research into the background of the organization to be saluted will indicate a pictorial design that will make a better showpiece than a letter or number. There are many sources of background information. Especially fertile fields are:

a. The history of the organization.

b. The purpose of work of the organization.

c. The mascot of the organization.

4. There are a few occasions when a letter or number formation is the only possibility. This is the reason for presenting the design techniques of the letter M.

THE ANCHOR   An important factor of formation design is symmetry. Many bandsmen can see the value and beauty of symmetry; but still the question of depicting something that has absolutely no symmetry often arises. Such items as a boat, shoe, boot, saddle, or profile cannot be presented in a symmetrical sense; therefore, they should be avoided. With some thought and planning a representative symmetrical figure for almost any class of subject can be found. As an example, it is far better to salute the Navy, or some other water-oriented group, with an anchor

Diagram 26 / **Formation design: Anchor**

KEY:

- ● Block position
- ⊙ Formation position
- ▣ Formation position of guide men

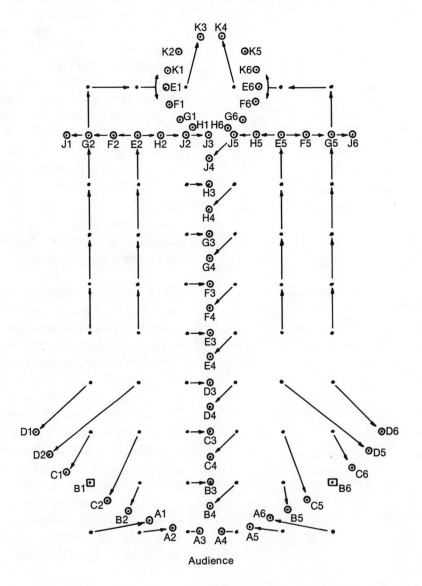

Audience

than attempt to design a nonsymmetrical boat formation. We shall illustrate an anchor formation using the same *procedures and techniques* as the pilot's wings formation. See *Diagram 26.*

1. General notes

   a. A sixty-man unit, six wide and ten deep, is used.

   b. The anchor sequence begins and ends in the block formation.

2. Footwork

   a. On the command of execution two mark-time steps are taken in place.

   b. B1 and B6 mark time and hold their block positions. These two members are the guide men for the hook of the anchor.

   c. A3 takes one left side step and marks time. A4 takes one right side step and marks time. Although these men move, they move so little that they can also be considered as guides for the hook.

   d. D1, D2, C1, C2, B2, A1, and A2 turn and proceed into their hook positions as shown in Diagram 26. Once in position, they turn to the audience and continue to mark time. This half of the anchor hook is established using B1 and A3 as guides. Two or three dry runs outside on this item will train the members for the routings and formation positions.

   e. D6, D5, C6, C5, B5, A6, and A5 turn and proceed into their hook positions as shown in the diagram. Once in position, they turn to the audience and continue to mark time. This curve is established by using B6 and A4 as guides.

   f. B3, C3, D3, E3, F3, G3, H3, and J3 take two left steps and continue to mark time. It is important that these members stay covered filewise, because they establish the first section of the stem of the anchor.

   g. B4, C4, D4, E4, F4, G4, H4, and J4 mark time two steps, then turn and proceed into position as shown and mark time. The men listed in f. (above) will be in position to serve as guides. In order to avoid a binding situation with the instruments, the men listed in f. and g. should be angled right and left alternately. All the number three men in the stem should, once in position, turn outward 45 degrees to the left, and the number four men in the stem, once in position, should turn outward 45 degrees to the right.

   h. J1 takes two right side steps and marks time.

   i. J6 takes two left side steps and marks time.

   j. K2 steps off to the left and, one pace later, executes a left flank. He then turns in, as shown, and begins the curve in the "eye" circle of the anchor. When in final position, he turns to the audience and marks time. K1 follows K2 as indicated.

   k. K3 executes to the rear and goes into position as per the diagram. He then turns to the audience and marks time.

   l. E1, F1, G1, and H1 execute to the rear and step off. Each one, in turn, executes an improvised right flank on the block position of K1 and then proceeds into his position in the "eye" as shown. Once in position, each man turns to the audience and marks time. This circle, although not difficult, must be considered a complex part of the anchor and will need a few walk-throughs to fix the procedure in the minds of the musicians. The other half of the "eye" is formed in a similar manner with the exception of turn directions.

m. J2 steps off to the left into position, as shown (two steps), turns front, and marks time—or J2 can execute four left side steps.

n. E2, F2, G2, and H2 execute to the rear and step off. When H2 reaches the block position of J2, he must execute an improvised right flank and take one step beyond the point of turn. He then turns to the audience and marks time. G2 and F2 execute a left flank on the block position of J2. G2 takes two paces after the point of turn, while F2 takes one pace beyond the point of turn. They then turn to the audience and mark time here. E2 moves into the block position of J2, turns to the audience, and marks time. This is the left half of the crossbar.

o. The right half of the crossbar is formed simultaneously, as shown in the diagram. It is important that the members of the crossbar use J1 and J6 as guides and establish a straight line between them.

3. Notes on the anchor formation.

a. All members face the bottom of the anchor or audience with the exception of the men in the stem, who are angled out alternately, 45 degrees right and left.

b. When the anchor is completely formed, and all the members are facing the audience and marking time, the mark time should be halted. The halt can be accomplished by coordination with a musical cue or by a signal from the drum major.

c. There are only two stationary guides, B1 and B6, but they are in strategic places. A number of the other members move such a short distance from their block positions that they can also be considered guides.

d. The block is reformed in the reverse manner, with the members paying attention to file number three, which resumes its block position in two side steps.

e. The arrows show the direction from the block positions into the anchor formation positions. The letter and number designations indicate the anchor formation position of each member.

f. The entire block formation is represented by dots. However, the block formation positions of certain men are occupied in the anchor formation by other men. (Note the anchor position of G2, who is occupying the block position of J1, etc.)

THE LONGHORN STEER   The longhorn steer could be used as a symbol in a salute to Texas. The steer's head is as representative as a star or a large T and more representative than a saddle or an entire steer. The design has meaning, simplicity, and clarity. The precision and symmetrical formation create a very interesting picture while it is being formed and broken. Again, symmetry is stressed because more clarity and definition can be obtained. See *Diagram 27.*

1. General notes

a. A sixty-man unit is used to show that good formation definition is possible with a limited number of musicians.

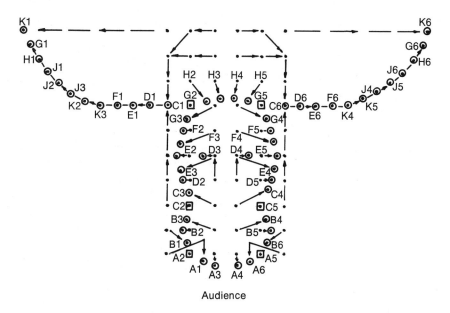

Diagram 27 / **Formation design: Longhorn Steer**

KEY:

●   Block position

◎   Formation position

▣   Formation position of guide men

Audience

b. The longhorn sequence begins and ends in block formation.

2. Footwork

a. On the command of execution two mark-time steps are made in place.

b. K1 steps out at a right angle to file one for twelve established paces.

c. G1 steps out at a right angle to file one for six established paces, then curves right as shown on Diagram 27 to establish the curve of the left horn.

d. H1 and J1 march straight ahead to the block position of G1. There each must execute an improvised right flank and follow the path generated by G1. The spacing between members is three-fourths of the established interval.

e. J2 and J3 step off to the right. Each executes a left flank at the block position of J1 and follows J1 into position in the horn.

f. K2 marks time four steps, then steps off 45 degrees to the right to the block position of J1, where K2 executes a half left and follows J3 into the left horn.

g. K3 marks time four steps, then steps off 90 degrees to the right to the block position of K2, executes a half left, and follows K2 into the left horn.

h. C1, D1, E1, and F1 execute to the rear and then mark time in their block positions until K3 turns on the block position of G1, at which time they step off in file, each executing a left flank on the block position of G1. They close to within three-fourths of the established interval of each other in the horn. Note that this will put C1 in G1's block position.

i. The guide men in the left half of the longhorn formation are G2, C2, and A2. They occupy the same position in the longhorn formation that they occupied in the block formation.

j. H2 and H3 move into formation as shown in the diagram.

Their exact longhorn position can be determined if they pay attention to G2.

k. F2 takes one right side step.

l. G3 proceeds into his longhorn position by the route shown. He has a perfect guide in G2 and F2.

m. E2 takes three right side steps.

n. F3 goes into his position as illustrated in the diagram. His guides are F2 and E2, both in position ahead of him.

o. D2 takes one right side step.

p. E3 goes into his position as illustrated. His guides are E2 and D2, who are in position ahead of him.

q. C3 goes into position as the diagram indicates. His guides are D2 and C2.

r. B2 takes one right side step.

s. B3 proceeds into formation as the diagram shows. His guides are C2 and B2.

t. B1 goes into position as illustrated. His guides are B2 and A2.

u. A1 takes the route shown. He utilizes A2 and A3 as guides.

v. A3 takes one half pace forward.

w. D3 executes to the rear and takes two paces to the block position of E3. There he executes an improvised left flank, and takes one half step in the new direction. As an alternative, D3 can take four steps backward, then one right side step, which will put him in the same position.

x. This completes the left side of the longhorn formation. The right side is executed in the same manner, with the exception of the turn direction.

3. Notes on the longhorn formation

a. All members turn to face the drum major as soon as they are in the longhorn formation or all can face front simultaneously on a music cue.

b. All members halt their mark-time step on a musical cue or a signal from the drum major.

c. The four members of the unit who have relatively difficult assignments are K1, K6, G1, and G6, who do the lead work to form the horns. It is suggested that these members should not play their instruments until they are in the longhorn formation. They should concentrate on forming the horns.

d. This formation has six guide men plus a large number of men who move only a step or two.

e. D3 and D4 are used for the "eyes" of the longhorn because they are the two bass drummers. These men do not stand facing the audience, but rather face each other, which gives the audience a side view of the bass drums. Thus, the eyes are as real in appearance as a band or drum corps can possibly portray them and, in addition, the rhythm beat is in the middle of the formation.

f. If a comic touch is desired following the music medley, two baton twirlers can run about ten feet of bright red crepe paper out of the mouth to suggest a tongue. The bass drummers can do a series of 360-degree turns in the spot in which they stand to mimic rolling eyes.

g. The block is reformed in the exact opposite manner. All routes back into the block formation are the same as those leading out.

NONSYMMETRICAL FORMATIONS   A symmetrical formation is a far better showpiece than a nonsymmetrical figure. In 95 percent of all cases a symmetrical design can be found for any kind of subject, but in some few cases the nonsymmetrical formation is the only possibility. The design procedures and techniques previously illustrated for symmetrical formations can be applied to nonsymmetrical works, but additional factors must be considered. The following design, selected for demonstration purposes, attempts to salute the "power age" on the anniversary of Watt's invention of the steam engine. The formation selected is a steam engine. Once the selection decision has been made, the question arises as to the type of steam engine. Shall it be a railroad engine, a stationary engine, horizontal or vertical type, etc.

The design should be as simple in structure as possible, even to the point of being austere. All extra appendages and corners should be eliminated. The extras do nothing but break lines of structure and give rise to doubt in the mind of the audience. For example, in the original sketching of a stationary steam engine, a design as follows might appear. See *Diagram 28, Sketch 1*. This sketch may seem absurd, but many designs are overcomplex and lose much of their identity primarily because of unnecessary appendages. It is very important *not* to use solid, heavy lines to connect the dots on a finished design drawing. *Sketch 1* is clear because of the solid outline. When the same formation is put on the field, where there are no solid connecting lines, the result may lack clarity. See *Diagram 28, Sketch 2*.

A close look at these sketches should prove that overcomplexity tends to confuse. To an audience this design would lack definition unless a commentary accompanied the formation. (The running commentary is a fine addition if properly used, but it should not be used to justify a formation. The commentary should complement the field work.) The same design idea can be presented with much greater clarity and force if details and appendages are kept to a minimum. The same steam engine could be designed with much greater definition. See *Diagram 28, Sketch 3*.

This sketch is a solid outline, but only for purposes of comparison. When this drawing is tranferred to actual member representation the picture is still clear. See *Diagram 28, Sketch 4*. All formations should be designed with simple lines in order to eliminate audience confusion and keep the bandsman's task relatively easy.

Another area of concern that is common to many nonsymmetrical formations is the use of animation or movement. Some movements

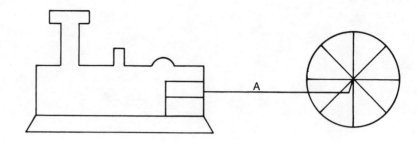

Diagram 28-1 / **Nonsymmetrical formation**

are quite simple and pose no difficulty, but many mechanical movements cannot be duplicated by members of a band. The various forms of animation which might be considered in design work are as follows;

1. *Angular motion.* This can best be described by an illustration. In the flywheel of the third and fourth sketches, the four spokes illustrate angular motion or angular rates of movement. In the rotation of the flywheel, each "spoke man" must use a different size step as his distance from the hub increases. In order to maintain a straight spoke the angular travel must be uniform. Uniform angular movement is not difficult to achieve with a little practice. The trick lies in the system of guide. The best guide to maintain straight spokes is a combination or cross-guide. This works in the following manner: The man in the outmost position of the spoke, i.e., the man farthest from the hub, sets the rate of rotation by marching with full established paces. No one else can set this pace properly. The remainder of the men in the spoke, whether they be two or ten, guide on him. This means they will always guide right for counterclockwise rotation. In the rotation of a figure such as this flywheel, care must be taken to avoid a rotation that is too slow. The outside men in the spoke or the men in the rim should set their movement at a full established pace in order to make the maneuver look alive and facilitate the guiding. If the outside men half-step or shuffle along, the guiding and alignment become more difficult and the effect of good animation is lost.

2. *Countermotion.* This is motion back and forth on a 180-degree change of direction. This motion is illustrated by the connecting rod labeled C in Sketches 3 and 4. The rod moves straight forward and backward. Many designers will attempt to create this motion by moving only the left leg of the bandsmen in the rod, forward—back-

Diagram 28-2 / **Nonsymmetrical formation**

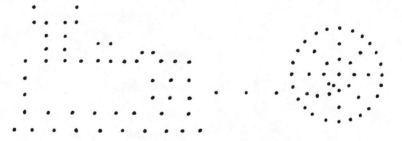

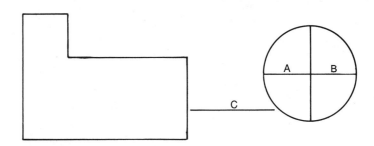

Diagram 28-3 / **Nonsymmetrical formation**

ward—forward, etc. This style of movement has two faults: First, the body or bulk of the man actually moves very little and therefore does not show definite countermotion. Second, the one leg motion is difficult from the point of view of the individual because of balance. In all countermotion the best method is to have one or two half-steps forward, followed by one or two half-steps backwards. This motion is easy for the musicians to maintain and looks very mechanical.

3. *Counter-angular-motion*. This motion should be avoided because it is impossible for a group to execute. Counter-angular-motion is illustrated by the action of the crank rod marked A- in Sketch 1. In the actual operation of a crank rod, this counter angular-motion is the true motion, but it cannot be executed in a representative manner by the bandsmen.

A third major point of trouble for a nonsymmetrical formation is the routing from block formation to the show formation. There is no visual balance of part and counterpart to aid the designer. As an example, let us consider forming the picture in Sketch 3.

We must now ask:

1. Will the design be recognized by the audience?

2. What section forms the boiler; what section forms the rod, and which the flywheel?

3. How is the block formation broken to form the design?

4. What routes will be taken into the show formation?

5. Where will the rhythm section be placed for visual and musical balance?

Diagram 28-4 / **Nonsymmetrical formation**

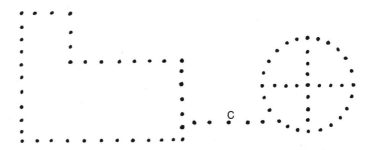

These questions pose problems and good solutions cannot always be found. In such cases, the use of an explosive type formation may be the easiest way out.

When all factors are considered, it becomes evident that the design and execution of nonsymmetrical formations are as difficult, and in most cases more difficult, than those of a symmetrical formation. In the odd cases where nonsymmetrical designs are the only alternatives, the wise planner and designer works toward simplification. He recognizes the inherent dangers of overcomplexity and complicated movement.

Remember, the preceding and following maneuvers and formations are to present procedures and techniques, illustrate the method of designing around obstacles and making maximum use of certain instruments such as tubas or bass drums in the formation. They are not blueprints for any existing organization. Once one masters technique there is almost no limit as to what can be designed for any type of marching musical unit.

*A study of
standard maneuvers
and formations*

**STANDARD MANEUVERS
AND FORMATIONS**

A library of standard maneuvers and formations should be just as important to the director as his library of standard music selections. The benefits the unit will gain from several standard maneuvers will outweigh many times the effort involved in perfecting them. It is no easy task to develop a good standard such as a company front or an operation scatter. The design is difficult, the music can be demanding and the footwork very intricate. Perfecting a standard maneuver requires a long-range program, not several two-hour practice sessions.

Characteristics of standard maneuvers and formations.

1. They have no regional, seasonal, or ethnic significance. They are used to show off the proficiency of the marching unit, to entertain an audience, or to pile up points in a competition.

2. They can be inserted in a show anywhere because they begin and end in the block formation and therefore are independent of other maneuvers and formations.

3. They should be rehearsed and retained in a ready or near-ready status so they can be used on short notice.

The advantages of standard maneuvers and formations:

1. They can be used again and again and actually become a trademark or signature of the unit. As an example, a band might open all of its field performances with a standard formation which dissolves into the block formation during a brilliant fanfare.

2. They enable the unit to present a revised field show more often than the alloted practice time indicates would be possible.

3. They enable the unit to respond to short notices with high-quality performances.

4. They set very high goals for the members and that infects other aspects of the unit's operation.

5. They cannot be perfected during the peak season; therefore, provide meaningful practice goals in the off season.

Standard maneuvers and formations can be used to great advantages under many conditions. If a unit has several standards perfected, it has a great advantage over its rivals that do not. To be more specific, we shall show how a band with four standard maneuvers might operate over a three-week period. In this example, the four standards are a fanfare opening, a company front, operation scatter, and an exit maneuver.

First week: Open with fanfare; use company front facing visitors; salute the visitors with a nonstandard formation; reverse the field and salute the home section with a nonstandard formation; leave the opposite end of the field with a big musical ending and a standard exit.

Second week: Fanfare from opposite end of field; company front facing home section; reverse the field and use new nonstandard formation saluting visitors; reverse the field and salute the home section with a nonstandard formation; exit opposite end of the field with standard exit.

Third week: Fanfare opening; replace company front with operation scatter; salute visitors with new, nonstandard formation; etc.

In the weeks following, the show may be changed by using new music for the various standard formations and maneuvers. This gives more time to develop a new salute to the visitors and to stress precision for standard maneuvers. Remember that precision is an ingredient that will win audiences anywhere in the world.

The director who has a library of perfected standards at his disposal, even though they may be limited in number, never need worry about a bad performance by his marching musical unit.

TURNS   Turning a marching musical unit 90 degrees right or left is the most common maneuver encountered in parades and field work. Many band and drum corps musicians, when asked to explain how a right or left turn is executed, are surprised that they actually do not understand the mechanics. Since turns require time for execution and are subject to audience reaction, they should be made into movements of precision, movements that hold the attention of the audience, movements that advertise the unit as being disciplined and proficient.

Although turns can be mastered with relatively little practice, the members must understand the footwork and rehearse the required steps. Two types of turns will be diagrammed and explained to illustrate that the 90-degree change of direction can be made into a good maneuver which will impress an audience.

90-degree turn—type A   This example is a left turn for a sixty-man unit. Once it is understood, the right turn can also be quickly mastered. See *Diagram 29*. The unit is moving along in a parade, and the drum major signals for a left turn. On the command of execution the A6 man makes a left flank movement and continues to march at a full pace. Two paces after the command of execution A5 makes a left flank and continues to march at a full pace. A4 takes four paces forward after the command of execution is given, executes a left flank, then continues at a full pace, and so on. A1 takes ten full paces forward following the command of execution, makes a left flank, and continues at a full pace.

If the unit is in a parade, the A6 man of this sixty-man unit should take twenty full paces immediately following his left flank movement and then come to a half step. As each man reaches his rank position following the turn, he should begin to march at a half step. When the block is reformed, the drum major can signal "Forward—March."

When the unit is performing on a football field A6 takes twenty full paces forward after his left flank and then marks time or half-steps as predetermined by the program format. Once the turn is completed and the block reformed, the drum major can give the appropriate baton cue to continue the performance.

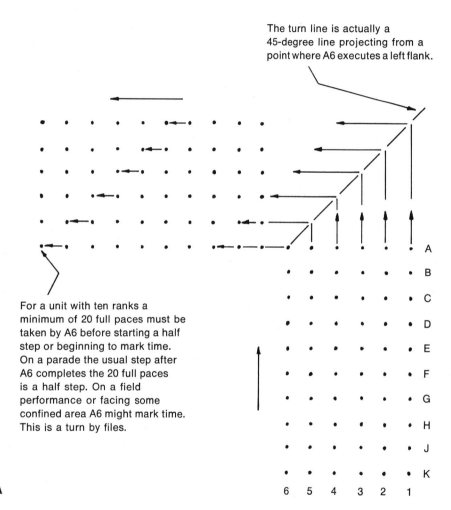

The turn line is actually a 45-degree line projecting from a point where A6 executes a left flank.

For a unit with ten ranks a minimum of 20 full paces must be taken by A6 before starting a half step or beginning to mark time. On a parade the usual step after A6 completes the 20 full paces is a half step. On a field performance or facing some confined area A6 might mark time. This is a turn by files.

Diagram 29 / **90-degree left turn—Type A**

NOTES ON THE 90-DEGREE TURN—TYPE A:

1. This type of turn is made by files.

2. This turn is normally entered while the unit is in block formation, with depth and lateral intervals of two established paces. The unit will then emerge from the turn with the same intervals. However, there are two variations:

a. If the unit goes into this type of turn in close formation it automatically emerges from the turn in block formation. (This knowledge is very useful in designing field shows.)

b. If the unit is in block formation and it is desired to execute a 90-degree left turn and emerge in close formation, it can be accomplished. Instead of each man in the A rank executing his left flank two paces after the man immediately on his left, as described earlier, each executes a left flank one pace after the man on his left. This reduces the interval to one pace between any two adjacent members of the A rank. Since this type of turn is made by files, the B, C, D, etc., ranks emulate the action just described for A. (Because the men flank on each consecutive step, A5, A3, and A1 must use the improvised left flank procedure. This is necessary because they reach their flank points as a left foot strikes the ground.) Using this procedure the unit enters the left turn in block formation and emerges in close formation. The same procedure, with the exception of the turn direction and the men who must use the improvised flank movement, can be used for a 90-degree right turn.

3. This type of turn is limited to 90 degrees. Should it be attempted on less or more than 90 degrees, the interval between files (rank intervals) would be destroyed. In a 45-degree turn, for example, the intervals between the files would increase. In a 120-degree turn, the intervals between files would decrease.

4. Once the command of execution is given for a left turn and A6 turns, the guide shifts from the stem of the T to the number six file. After the completion of the turn the guide shifts back to the T on the "Forward—March" signal.

5. Only the A men must count steps. Each man in the A rank counts one—two after the point at which the man on his left executes a left flank. The men in each file turn at the same point as the A man of their file.

6. K1 is the member who governs the time required for this left turn, since he is the last member to regain his block position. The drum major should not signal for any action until K1 has completed his turn and the unit is aligned.

7. *Diagram 29* shows that the turning points (left flank points) project 45 degrees counterclockwise from the original line held by A rank. This gives the effect of a series of increasing and diminishing V's where both the file and rank intervals are maintained during the entire turn.

8. The *right* turn is equally simple, except that A1 would right-flank on the command of execution and A6 would go forward ten full paces before making his right flank. The number of steps to the flanking point in the right turn differs for each man in the A rank. In the left turn, for example, A5 takes two paces forward after the command of execution before executing a left flank. In a right turn, he takes eight paces forward before he executes a right flank. See *Diagram 29*.

90-degree turn—type B   A type B turn can be used under more conditions than can type A. Type A is restricted to a 90-degree right or left turn. Type B can be used as follows:

1. On turns of more than or less than 90 degrees.

2. With the band in block formation or in close formation.

See *Diagram 30*. The unit is marching straight ahead and the drum major signals for a right turn. On the command of execution A1 executes a right flank and at the same instant A2, A3, A4, A5, and A6 execute a half right. *This turn is made by ranks instead of files.* After his right flank, A1 should step out twenty full paces, then, if on a parade, begin a half step. On a field performance he might mark time. When A2 executes a half right, he has about two and one half steps to go before he must execute another half right. This means A2 must use a combination of short and long paces. All of the number two file men must go through this routine. The lengths of the 45-degree legs are different for each file, but none of these leg lengths is an exact number of paces. This prevents the turn from being precise. The B rank turns where the A rank turned and then follows A's exact procedure. Ranks C, D, E, etc., do likewise. Since it is impossible to perfect this type of turn, it must be considered a necessary evil of maneuvering. It should be employed only when the use of the A type turn is an impossibility.

Diagram 30 / **90-degree right turn—Type B**

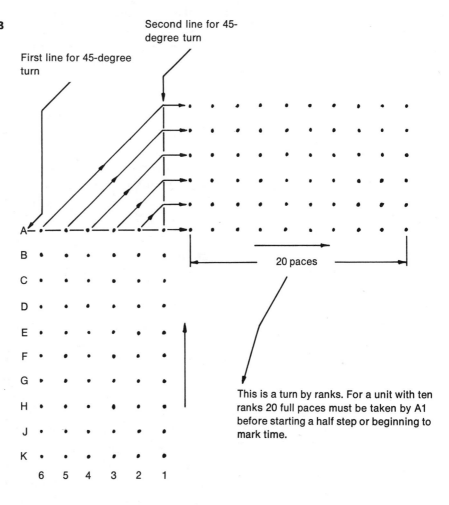

First line for 45-degree turn

Second line for 45-degree turn

20 paces

This is a turn by ranks. For a unit with ten ranks 20 full paces must be taken by A1 before starting a half step or beginning to mark time.

NOTES ON THE 90-DEGREE TURN—TYPE B:

1. This type turn is made by ranks.

2. On the command of execution the guide shifts from the T to the men in the right file. It remains there until the next signal is given by the drum major. The guide then shifts back to the T.

3. The 45-degree lines of march should be straight. A majority of bandsmen will tend to curve these lines, causing the unit to emerge from the turn with its width interval closed up to something less than the established interval.

4. See *Diagram 30*. The same mechanics used for the execution of the right turn, type B, should be used for the left turn, type B.

5. This type of turn is a compromise; it is impossible to perfect it, but it can move a marching unit around a corner in a relatively orderly manner.

CLOSE AND OPEN INTERVAL MANEUVERS

Close interval is the maneuver whereby the space between files of a unit is decreased from the established interval to one half of the established interval. This movement can be an effective showpiece when executed correctly. The explanation makes use of a sixty-member unit.

The steps necessary to move to a close interval formation and then open up to an established interval or the block formation will be explained in two specific examples. Example number one illustrates closing and opening the interval while on the march. Example number two illustrates closing and opening the interval while standing at attention. In both examples the unit should close on the stem of the T, or file number three. This will raise the question of closing to the exact center, which means closing on the space between files three and four. This is possible, but closing the unit on the stem of the T will be more exact and look sharper since the guide is fixed there. *A cardinal rule should be: Never sacrifice or compromise the guide element if it can be prevented.* For these maneuvers it actually would be better to have an odd number of files in the unit, since this would give an exact center file to close on. (This is a rare instance where a unit would benefit from an odd number of files, but remember that symmetrical formations are impossible for a unit with an odd number of files.)

Example number one

1. Close interval while on the march

a. The unit can be playing music or marching to a drum tap.

b. The sixty-man unit is moving forward in block formation; the command of execution should be given as the left foot strikes the ground.

c. The stem of the T, or all number three men, begin a half step.

d. Files one and two immediately (on the next right foot) execute a left oblique. They maintain a full step and close in on the number three men of their respective ranks until a one-pace lateral interval is established. They then execute a right oblique and, when aligned with the number three man in their rank, begin a half step.

e. Files four, five, and six execute an improvised right oblique and continue at a full step until the one-pace lateral interval is established. They then execute a left oblique and when they are aligned with the number three man in their rank, they begin a half step.

f. Another manner in which this can be done is to have files four, five, and six take one step ahead after the command of execution and then perform a right oblique. This alternate method is not nearly as effective as the first, because the movement is not completely spontaneous.

g. The drum major can signal "Forward—March" when the entire unit is in close formation and at a half step.

h. Notice that the two-pace interval in depth or from rank to rank remains.

i. See *Diagram 31*.

j. Note the drum major's signal.

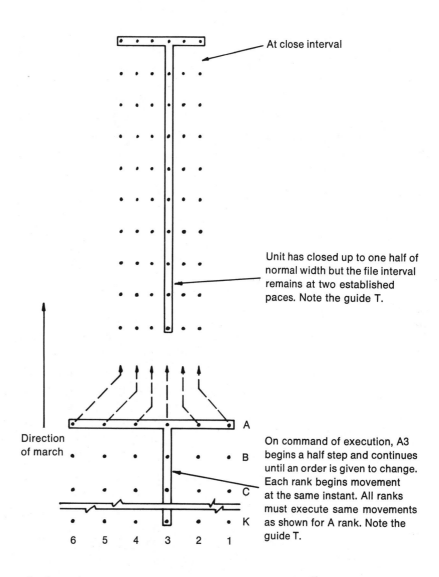

At close interval

Unit has closed up to one half of normal width but the file interval remains at two established paces. Note the guide T.

Direction of march

On command of execution, A3 begins a half step and continues until an order is given to change. Each rank begins movement at the same instant. All ranks must execute same movements as shown for A rank. Note the guide T.

A
B
C
K

6   5   4   3   2   1

Diagram 31 / **Close interval maneuver while marching**

2. Open interval while on the march

a. The unit can be playing music or marching to a drum tap.

b. The unit is moving forward at close interval; the command of execution should be given as the left foot strikes the ground.

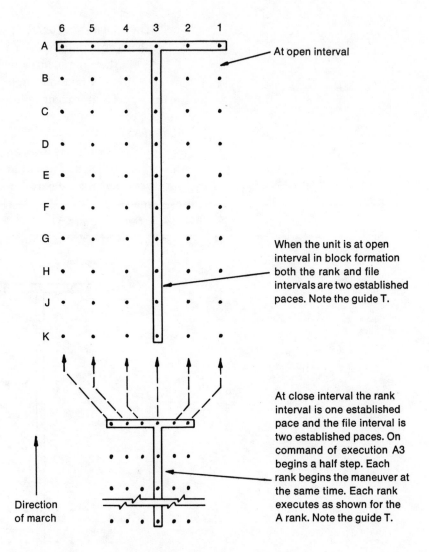

Diagram 32 / **Open interval maneuver while marching** /

Direction of march

At open interval

When the unit is at open interval in block formation both the rank and file intervals are two established paces. Note the guide T.

At close interval the rank interval is one established pace and the file interval is two established paces. On command of execution A3 begins a half step. Each rank begins the maneuver at the same time. Each rank executes as shown for the A rank. Note the guide T.

c. The stem of the T begins a half step.

d. Files one and two execute an improvised right oblique and continue at a full step until they attain the established rank interval. They then execute a left oblique and when aligned with the number three men in their rank begin a half step.

e. Files four, five, and six execute a left oblique and march out until the established interval between files is attained. They execute a right oblique and when aligned begin a half step. The drum major can give "Forward—March" or any predetermined signal to continue the march or performance.

f. See *Diagram 32.*

g. Note drum major's signal.

3. Notes on close and open interval while on the march:

a. These maneuvers must be executed correctly if the unit is to be considered well trained.

b. They can be performed as precise maneuvers while marching with or without music.

c. The improvised obliques must be used to effect simultaneous and coordinated breaks. Regardless of the foot on which the command is given, only one section will be permitted to execute a legitimate oblique at the proper time. The improvised oblique will allow simultaneous execution of both oblique directions. The organization will look much more polished if all obliquing files break at the same time.

d. The close and open interval movements become display maneuvers when executed correctly.

Example number two

1. Close interval from the position of standing attention

It often happens that an organization in block formation waiting for a function to begin will be forced to permit official traffic to pass. Mass formations with other units on a performance field often require the width of the organizations to be decreased. Many such situations require that the band be narrowed to close interval, and it must be put there from the position of standing attention. There are many ways of making this change, but only one good method. When the unit must be moved because of traffic, it is easy to crowd the members onto one side of the street by yelling at them. It is *almost as easy* to call the band to attention, order "Close Interval—March" and, once it is at close interval, side-step it out of the way. This is showmanship and indicates an elite organization that takes advantage of every little opportunity to demonstrate its capability. The action is as follows:

a. The organization is in block formation, at attention, not playing music; the demand is "Close interval—March."

b. The stem of the T, file three, marks time.

c. File two takes two left side steps.

d. File one takes four left side steps.

e. File four takes two right side steps.

f. File five takes four right side steps.

g. File six takes six right side steps.

h. See *Diagram 33a.*

i. Note drum major's signal.

All side-step movements are begun simultaneously. This puts the unit at close interval. It is a good idea to use drum taps for cadence during the maneuver; it adds an edge of sharpness. The only rehearsal necessary for this maneuver is to train the files to stay covered as they side-step.

Diagram 33a / **Side step to close interval from the position of standing attention at open interval** On the command of execution all ranks execute simultaneously as shown for rank A.

KEY:

● Open interval (beginning of maneuver)

◉ Close interval (completion of maneuver)

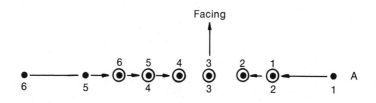

2. Open interval from the position of standing attention

a. The organization is at close interval, at attention, not playing music; the command is "Open interval—March."

b. The stem of the T, file three, marks time.

c. File two takes two right side steps.

d. File one takes four right side steps.

e. File two takes two right side steps.

f. File four takes two left side steps.

g. File five takes four left side steps.

h. File six takes six left side steps. (This returns the unit to block formation.)

i. See *Diagram 33b*.

j. Note drum major's signal.

Diagram 33b / **Side step to open interval from the position of standing attention at close interval** On the command of execution all ranks execute simultaneously as shown for rank A.

KEY:

● Close interval (beginning of maneuver)

◉ Open interval (completion of maneuver)

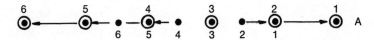

NOTE: When the bandsmen reach the close interval position they should mark time until halted by the drum major. Likewise, when the bandsmen reach the open interval position they should mark time until halted by the drum major. This allows time for alignment and also permits the use of an exaggerated halt to dramatize the unit's overall proficiency.

THE BOX REVERSE

There is an excellent maneuver that accomplishes a 180-degree change of direction for a marching unit. It is the box reverse. It is more precise and spectacular than the much-used countermarch. From ground level or high in the stadium, the observer sees a countermarch as a milling scene which he must endure because a 180-degree change of direction is necessary. A countermarch consumes time and during that time the unit may lose the attention of a great part of its audience. In addition, the countermarch requires a clearance in front of the A rank almost equal to the width of the unit in order to allow for proper execution. Many directors have recognized the deficiencies of the countermarch and have attempted to remedy the visual and space problems. Some have tried turning each file led by the A rank into the opening immediately to the left and thereby change the direction of the unit 180 degrees. This solves the extra space problem and the maneuver can be very precise; however, the unit emerges with the guide disoriented; therefore it is not feasible.

The box reverse boasts the following advantages:

1. The unit's direction can be changed 180 degrees on the exact area occupied by the block formation.

2. The unit emerges with its guide elements oriented exactly as they entered the maneuver.

3. It is very interesting for the spectators because it is a precision maneuver.

4. The box reverse appears to be a complicated maneuver but in reality it is easily performed. See *Diagram 34*, which shows a box reverse for a sixty-piece unit.

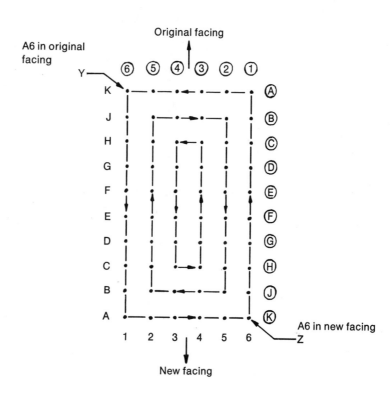

Diagram 34 / **Box Reverse for a 60-man unit** Purpose: To change direction 180 degrees. Notes: 1. Turn uses independent countermoving rectangles. 2. Arrows indicate direction of movement.

KEY:

Ⓐ,①, etc.   Positions before the maneuver

A, 1, etc.   Positions after the maneuver

NOTES ON THE BOX REVERSE:

1. The "reverse" is made utilizing a series of rectangles. The rectangles are outlined in the diagram by dotted lines.

2. The arrows on the diagram show that the direction of rotation of any rectangle is opposite of its neighbor. All rectangles could rotate in the same direction, but counter-rotation presents more effective animation.

3. All turns and intervals should be exact. The pivot points on the corners of all rectangles should be carefully observed so that they will not drift as the men turn.

4. The command of execution should come on the right foot. All members who must execute to the rear do so immediately on the next left foot. All members who must either turn right or left to begin the rectangle circuit turn the necessary direction on the first left foot after the command of execution, mark time one step, and then step off. For

these members who must turn right or left, the sequence is: right foot (command of execution); left foot (pivot in necessary direction); right foot (set beside left in mark time); left foot (step off on path around rectangle). In other words, after the command of execution two steps are necessary to get the rectangles oriented so that they can rotate. The next left foot (third step) should be the step-off, where all rectangles move in the designated rotation. All members who must turn right or left mark time, or kill one step, to permit the men who execute to the rear to begin the rectangular movement properly. This permits exact established intervals to be maintained in the rectangular movement.

5. This maneuver can begin while on the march, from a mark time, or from a halt.

The outside rectangle in Diagram 34 operates in the following manner:

1. On the command of execution, all of file number six, except K6, must execute to the rear.

2. The K rank, except for K1, turns right and marks time for one step. The step immediately following the command of execution (or the time of execution step) is a pivot step. The right foot is set down beside the left immediately after the pivot. This one mark-time step is absolutely essential for those members who must turn right or left.

3. File one, except for A1, marks time one step. The command of execution is given on the right foot. The left foot is then advanced, the right is set beside it, and the step-off is made with the left.

4. Rank A, except for A6, should pivot left and mark time one step. At this moment (after the mark-time step) all men in the outside rectangle step off. They should pay close attention to their intervals and pivot points as they rotate. When A6 has moved from his original position, marked Y in the diagram, to his new position, marked Z, all the other members of the outside rectangle will be in their new positions.

5. After the rotation has been completed, all members in the outside rectangle with the exception of A1 through J1 of file number one are facing in the wrong direction. These men must turn so that all face the new direction of march. Each man turns individually as soon as he reaches his new position. All continue to mark time.

6. All of the rectangles maneuver (with exception of turn direction) in the exact manner described for the largest or outside rectangle. Since the outside rectangle must travel a greater distance than the others, it will be positioned last. As soon as the drum major sees the outside rectangle reoriented he knows that the inner rectangles, too, have completed their part in the box reverse.

7. The drum major should march around the outside of the band while the rectangles are turning. By the time the unit has completed the 180-degree reverse, he is in position.

8. The box reverse maneuver will work for any size unit having an even number of files. See *Diagram 35*, which shows a box reverse for a ninety-six-piece unit.

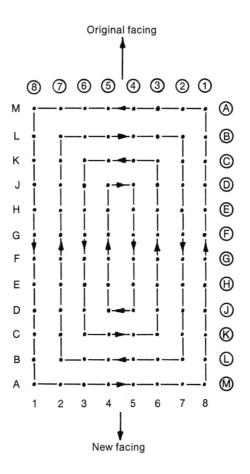

Diagram 35 / **Box Reverse for a 96-man unit**

KEY:

Ⓐ,① , etc. Positions before the maneuver

A, 1, etc. Positions after the maneuver

THE WALTZ Most marching musical bands use some type of dance step as a maneuver. Attempts have been made to execute the rhumba, fox trot, tango, waltz, and samba with varying degrees of success and audience appeal. A dance step can be a good maneuver, but care must be taken when selecting the dance and planning the footwork and the music. Not all dance steps are suitable for performance by a band.

There are many factors that must be considered in the design of such a maneuver. The major items of concern are:

1. Step. The step must not be more complicated than can be successfully mastered by the bandsman. One dance step that can be executed with precision is a slow waltz step.

2. Music. The music selected must allow for precision execution of the steps. It must be remembered that the band members must play the music, execute the steps, and maintain alignment.

3. Formation. A good formation in which to execute the dance step is the block formation. If the dance is spread over too great an area, its use as a standard is limited. For example, if the dance is scattered over a football field the maneuver could not be used as a showpiece at the reviewing stand in a parade.

The mechanics of the waltz   The unit must be at attention and in block formation to begin the waltz. A thirty-inch established pace is assumed for this example. The drum major, facing the band, raises his baton and sets the tempo with a baton signal. The music *must* be a slow waltz. It can be arranged so as to have a very short introduction, during which time the unit should hold at attention. On the first beat of the chorus the members step out on a waltz pattern. One waltz pattern, which is executed in three parts, follows:

PART ONE   The entire unit steps out fifteen inches, at 45 degrees to the left, on the first beat of the chorus. The right foot is brought up beside the left on the second beat. The unit holds fast during the third beat. On the first beat of the second bar, each member steps out fifteen inches at 45 degrees to the right. On the second beat, the left foot is brought up beside the right. The unit holds fast during the third beat. On the first beat of the third bar, each member steps backward fifteen inches at 45 degrees to the right. The men hold fast during the third beat. On the first beat of the fourth bar, each member steps backward fifteen inches at 45 degrees to the left. The unit holds fast on the third beat. At this point, all members are back at their starting positions. Four bars are required to execute the box step. See *Diagram 36*, part one.

PART TWO   On the first beat of the fifth bar, the right foot of each member is placed straight back fifteen inches. The members roll forward on the second beat and hold fast on the third. During the sixth bar, the members, without lifting their feet, roll back on the first beat, roll forward on the second, and hold on the third. The steps of the seventh bar are identical to those of the fifth and sixth. During the eighth bar, the men roll back on the first step, roll forward on the second, and at the same time bring the right foot up beside the left. All hold fast on the third beat. At this point, each man should be back at his starting point. The box step, part one; and the roll back, part two, are repeated. The two parts of the waltz just described required eight bars of music for one complete execution, sixteen bars when repeated. See *Diagram 36*, part two.

PART THREE   On the first beat of the seventeenth bar, files one, two, and three, A through K, step out fifteen inches at 45 degrees to the right, On the second beat, the left foot is brought up beside the right, and all hold fast during the third. Concurrently, files four, five, and six perform as follows: On the first beat of the seventeenth bar they step out fifteen inches at 45 degrees to the left. On the second beat, the right foot is brought up beside the left, and all hold fast during the third. These actions cause the entire unit to open down the middle between files four and three. Half of the unit goes to the right and the other half goes to the left. On the first beat of the eighteenth bar, files one, two, and three step out fifteen inches at 45 degrees to the left. On the second beat, the right foot is brought up beside the left, and all hold fast on the third. Concurrently, files four, five, and six perform as follows: On the first beat they step out fifteen inches at 45 degrees to the right.

On the second beat the left foot is brought up beside the right, and all hold fast on the third. This again places the entire unit in block formation. This out-and-in, "sawtooth" procedure can be repeated as often as desired. When the desired repeats have been made, the unit should halt in block formation and complete the music with some full-sounding chords. See *Diagram 36*, part three.

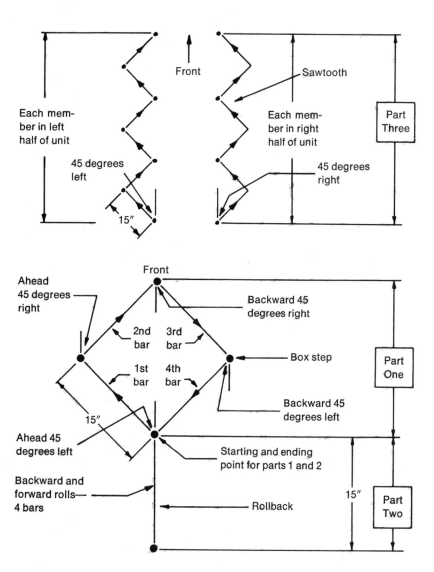

Diagram 36 / **The waltz**

NOTES ON THE WALTZ:

1. The waltz tempo must be slow.

2. The box step, part one, shows, by the hesitation on the third beat, a definite visual rhythm pattern. The roll-back, part two, shows the smooth movement of the waltz.

3. The sawtooth movement, part three, shows the visual rhythm pattern again.

4. During parts one and two the unit requires little more space than the block coverage to maneuver, since the members end up at exactly

the same place they started. During part three the organization moves slowly forward.

5. Since the movement begins and ends in the block formation, it can be inserted in a performance at almost any point desired.

6. Alignment is the difficult requirement for the bandsmen.

7. A movie of a single individual executing the steps is very useful for training purposes.

8. The waltz pattern can be painted on the rehearsal room floor to assist the bandsmen with the footwork. (Always take advantage of little training aids. Such aids not only fix the mechanics of a maneuver in the minds of the men but they are also constant reminders that the unit is aiming at perfection.)

OPERATION SCATTER   There are many good standard maneuvers but only a few that can be classed as great. One such great maneuver is operation scatter. Operation scatter is a spectacle. It can be precise to the point of absolute perfection. It depicts nothing but it can prove that the unit is extremely well trained and polished. A great amount of work is required to perfect it, and unless it is worked out to near-perfection, it is not advisable to use it at all. The area necessary for the maneuver is sixteen established paces plus the width of the block formation and thirty-two established paces plus the block length. Operation scatter is very short in duration, lasting thirty-four steps from the time the block formation breaks until the block is reformed. There are many good sixteen-bar percussion solos that can be used to set the maneuver cadence and there are many good marches in which a sixteen-bar percussion solo can be inserted. The cadence for operation scatter should consist of a percussion section solo of sixteen bars, rather than sixteen bars of music by the entire unit for several reasons:

1. The break in the music and the introduction of the percussion solo invites attention.

2. It allows the greater part of the unit to pay strict attention to the footwork of the maneuver.

3. The percussion solo can be divided into phases of four bars each, with a very distinct pick-up for each phase. The pick-up serves as the command for the execution of each phase of the maneuver and thus eliminates the necessity of counting steps. See *Diagram 37.*

Operation scatter is a continuous movement, but to clarify each of the four phases it is necessary to use a series of four diagrams. On each diagram the original position of the block, the position of the members at the end of that particular phase, the routes in that phase, and the routes to the next phase are all illustrated. The phase diagrams must be studied, since they illustrate distances, lines of march, flankings, and other elements.

A broad description of the maneuver is as follows: The unit is proceeding down the field, playing a march. At an appropriate place in the march, the percussion solo can be inserted. On the first beat of the percussion solo, operation scatter is begun and continues for thirty-two

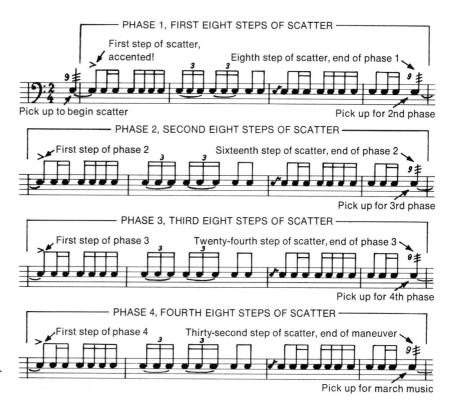

Diagram 37 / **Percussion solo for operation scatter**

steps. At the end of the percussion solo, or thirty-two steps later, the entire band picks up the march music. Only two steps are required, once the music is picked up, to return the unit to block formation. This is particularly effective because, at the moment the music begins, it appears that all of the separate elements of operation scatter will crash into each other. The fourth phase diagram, however, illustrates that two steps after the apparent collision, the block is reformed and moving down the field on its original line of march.

Each diagram shows several important factors:

1. Dots in each phase diagram represent the position of the original block formation at the beginning of the drum solo.

2. Circled dots show the position of each member's right foot at the end of that phase. In *Diagram 38*, for phase one, the circled dots show the position of each bandsman's right foot on the eighth step of the maneuver. In *Diagram 39*, for phase two, the circled dots show the position of each member's right foot on the sixteenth step, and so on.

3. A solid line, with an arrowhead, indicates the direction used to reach the circled dot position for each phase.

4. A dotted line, with an arrowhead, indicates the direction used to proceed into the next phase.

The first four bars, or eight steps (phase one), of operation scatter are executed as follows:

1. File one executes a right flank (two paces) and steps out six paces in the new direction, east. After the right flank the guide is right.

2. File two executes to the rear (two steps) and marches six paces in the new direction, south.

3. File three continues straight ahead for eight paces, north.

4. File four continues straight ahead for eight paces, north.

5. File five executes to the rear (two steps) and marches six paces in the new direction, south.

6. File six executes an improvised left flank (two paces) and steps out six paces in the new direction, west. After the improvised left flank the guide is left. In the first phase, file six must execute an improvised left flank, to permit it to break outward at the same instant as file one. This ends phase one. See *Diagram 38.*

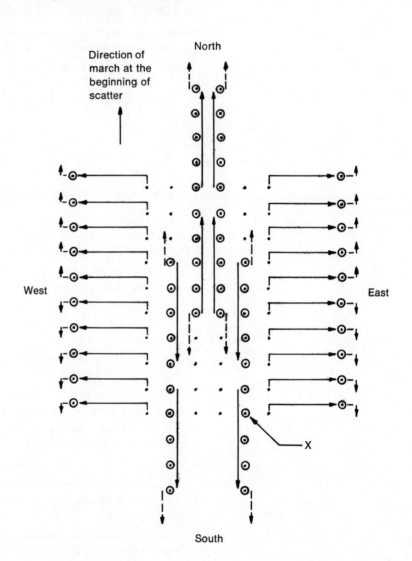

Diagram 38 / **Operation scatter: phase one**

KEY:

●   Block position of unit at beginning of scatter

X   Original block position of K2 occupied by G2 at the end of phase one

⊙   Position of right foot at the end of phase one, or the eighth step of scatter

◄—   Route taken into ⊙ position

◄--   Indicates route to be taken into phase two

The second four bars, or second eight steps (phase two), of operation scatter are executed as follows:

1. On steps nine and ten A1, B1, C1, D1, and E1 execute an improvised left flank (two steps) and then take six additional paces in the new direction, north. On steps nine and ten F1, G1, H1, J1, and K1 execute a right flank (two steps) and continue six more paces in the new direction, south.

2. On steps nine and ten A2, B2, C2, D2 and E2 execute to the rear (two steps) and continue six more paces in the new direction, north. F2, G2, H2, J2, and K2 continue eight paces in the same direction as in phase one, south.

3. A3, B3, C3, D3, and E3 continue eight paces in the same direction as in phase one, north. On steps nine and ten F3, G3, H3, J3, and K3 execute to the rear (two steps) and continue six more steps in the new direction, south.

4. A4, B4, C4, D4, and E4 continue eight paces in the same direction as in phase one, north. On steps nine and ten F4, G4, H4, J4, and K4 execute to the rear (two steps) and continue six more steps in the new ·direction, south.

Diagram 39 / **Operation scatter: phase two**

KEY:

- •   Original block position
- ⊙   Position of right foot at end of phase two, or sixteenth step of scatter
- ←   Route into ⊙ position
- ◄ - -   Route to be taken into phase three

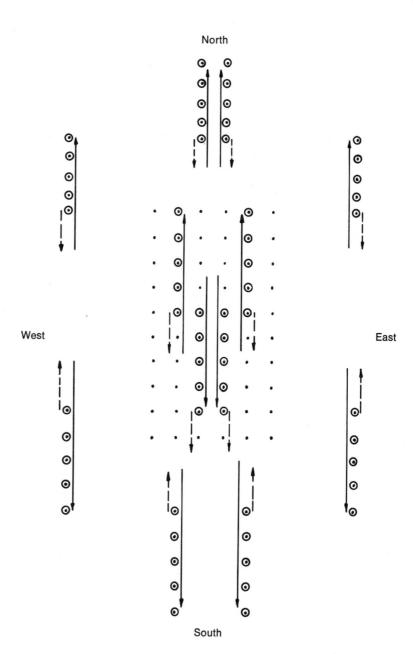

North

West

East

South

5. On steps nine and ten A5, B5, C5, D5, and E5 execute to the rear (two steps) and continue six more paces in the new direction, north. F5, G5, H5, J5, and K5 continue eight paces in the same direction as in phase one, south.

6. On steps nine and ten A6, B6, C6, D6, and E6 execute a right flank (two steps) and then continue six additional paces in the new direction, north. On steps nine and ten F6, G6, H6, J6, and K6 execute an improvised left flank (two steps) and then continue six more paces in the new direction, south. This ends phase two. See *Diagram 39.*

The third four bars, or third eight steps (phase three), of operation scatter are executed as follows:

1. On steps seventeen and eighteen A1, B1, C1, D1, and E1 execute to the rear (two steps) and then continue six more paces in the new direction, south. On steps seventeen and eighteen F1, G1, H1, J1, and K1 execute to the rear (two steps) and then continue six more paces in the new direction, north.

2. A2, B2, C2, D2, and E2 continue eight paces in the same direction

Diagram 40 / **Operation scatter: phase three**

KEY:

- •   Original block position
- ⊙   Position of the right foot at the end of phase three, or the twenty-fourth step of scatter
- ⭠   Route taken into ⊙ position
- ⭠--   Route to be taken into phase four

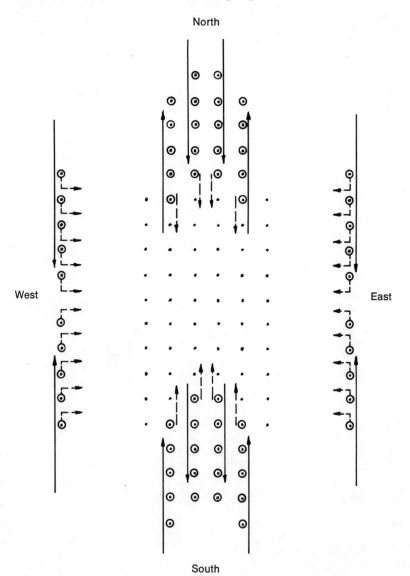

North

West

East

South

as in phase two, north. On steps seventeen and eighteen F2, G2, H2, J2, and K2 execute to the rear (two steps) and then continue six more paces in the new direction, north.

3. On steps seventeen and eighteen A3, B3, C3, D3, and E3 execute to the rear (two steps) and then continue six more paces in the new direction, south. F3, G3, H3, J3, and K3 continue eight paces in the same direction as in phase two, south.

4. On steps seventeen and eighteen A4, B4, C4, D4, and E4 execute to the rear (two steps) and then continue six more paces in the new direction, south. F4, G4, H4, J4, and K4 continue eight paces in the same direction as in phase two, south.

5. A5, B5, C5, D5, and E5 continue eight paces in the same direction as in phase two, north. On steps seventeen and eighteen of the maneuver F5, G5, H5, J5, and K5 execute to the rear (two steps) and then continue six more paces in the new direction, north.

6. On steps seventeen and eighteen of the maneuver, A6, B6, C6, D6, and E6 execute to the rear and then continue six more paces in the new direction, south. On steps seventeen and eighteen of the maneuver F6, G6, H6, J6, and K6 execute to the rear (two steps) and then continue six more paces in the new direction, north. This ends phase three. See *Diagram 40*.

The fourth four bars, or fourth eight steps (phase four), of operation scatter are executed as follows:

1. On steps twenty-five and twenty-six A1, B1, C1, D1, and E1 execute a right flank (two steps) and then continue six more paces in the new direction, west. On steps twenty-five and twenty-six F1, G1, H1, J1, and K1 execute an improvised left flank (two steps) and then continue six more paces in the new direction, west.

2. On steps twenty-five and twenty-six A2, B2, C2, D2, and E2 execute to the rear (two steps) and then continue six more steps in the new direction, south. F2, G2, H2, J2, and K2 continue eight paces in the same direction as in phase three, north.

3. A3, B3, C3, D3, and E3 continue eight paces in the same direction as in phase three, south. On steps twenty-five and twenty-six F3, G3, H3, J3, and K3 execute to the rear (two steps) and then continue six more paces in the new direction, north.

4. A4, B4, C4, D4, and E4 continue eight paces in the same direction as in phase three, south. On steps twenty-five and twenty-six F4, G4, H4, J4, and K4 execute to the rear (two steps) and then continue six more steps in the new direction, north.

5. On steps twenty-five and twenty-six A5, B5, C5, D5, and E5 execute to the rear (two steps), then continue six more paces in the new direction, south. F5, G5, H5, J5, and K5 continue eight paces in the same direction as in phase three, north.

6. On steps twenty-five and twenty-six A6, B6, C6, D6, and E6 execute an improvised left flank (two steps), then continue six more paces in the new direction, east. On steps twenty-five and twenty-six F6, G6, H6, J6, and K6 execute a right flank (two steps), then continue six additional paces in the new direction, east. This ends phase four. See *Diagram 41*.

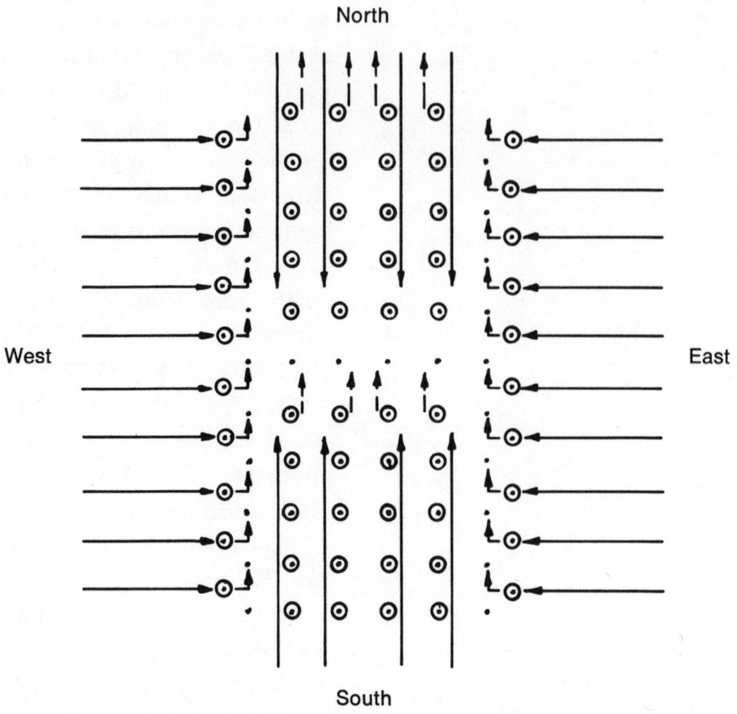

North

West

East

Diagram 41 / **Operation scatter: phase four**

KEY:

- • Original block position
- ⊙ Position of the right foot at the end of phase four, or the thirty-second step of scatter. The thirty-second step ends scatter but two additional steps are necessary to reform the block.
- ⟵ Route taken into ⊙ position
- ⟵-- Route to be taken to reform the block in two steps

South

The thirty-second step is the one that terminates the maneuver, but two additional steps are required to reform the block. To reform the block formation during the first two beats of the march music, the footwork is as follows:

1. On steps one and two of the march music, all of the number one men execute a right flank (two steps).

2. On steps one and two of the march music, A2, B2, C2, D2, and E2 execute to the rear (two steps). F2, G2, H2, J2, and K2 take two steps straight ahead.

3. On steps one and two of the march music, A3, B3, C3, D3, and E3 execute to the rear (two steps). F3, G3, H3, J3, and K3 take two steps straight ahead.

4. On steps one and two of the march music A4, B4, C4, D4, and E4 execute to the rear (two steps). F4, G4, H4, J4, and K4 take two steps straight ahead.

5. On steps one and two of the march music A5, B5, C5, D5, and E5 execute to the rear (two steps). F5, G5, H5, J5, and K5 take two steps straight ahead.

6. On steps one and two of the march music, all of the number six men execute an improvised left flank (two steps).

(At this point the entire block is reformed and is moving down the field in its original direction and centered as it was before the maneuver began.)

NOTES ON OPERATION SCATTER:

1. The frequent use of improvised flank movements in this maneuver is an absolute necessity in order to have all factions make and

break each phase simultaneously. Unless the makes and breaks are simultaneous, the maneuver is less than spectacular.

2. It is easy to see that the maneuver is performed by five-man elements in this sixty-man example. This is a good point to keep in mind during practice. Each group of five should spend some time practicing its part of the maneuver alone. During the maneuver each element actually operates completely independent.

3. The explanation is broken into phases but there is no hesitation in the maneuver—it moves continuously.

4. Cover, alignment, and the proper footwork must be stressed.

5. The most crucial moment of the entire operation is at the final, or thirty-second, step of the maneuver. At this point it appears that there is going to be a collision and yet, two steps later, the block is reformed and moving in its original line of march.

6. A varying pace during the maneuver will cause a great deal of trouble. The unit must have an established pace and interval.

7. Numbered steps such as eight, twenty-five, etc., are mentioned throughout the explanation of the footwork. This is merely for purposes of training and study. The maneuver can be executed without any counting if close attention is paid by all members to the percussion solo, which indicates the phase breaks.

8. Although we have used a sixty-member unit, the maneuver can be worked out for any size organization, once the principle is understood.

9. This is a difficult maneuver but it is a great standard. It can be used indefinitely, once it is perfected.

THE COMPANY FRONT   A company front consists of a single line of musicians with every member of the unit in that line facing the audience.

It is very impressive because it permits an unobstructed view of each man and directs the full power of the music directly at the audience. There are numerous techniques that can be used to form a company front. The formation and reform procedures used in this example hold the required maneuver area to a minimum. This permits its use in a field show or for a salute in front of a reviewing stand. Any maneuver that lends itself to different uses is especially valuable. This particular design provides both a useful and an all-occasion showpiece because:

1. The width of the area necessary to execute the maneuver is only 50 percent greater than the width of the block formation.

2. A great deal of animation takes place in a short time and the company front is in the spectacular class of maneuvers.

3. The block is reformed after the maneuver.

4. The same direction of march is maintained after the block is reformed.

A forty-eight-piece unit is used to illustrate the design technique for the company front. It would not add to the clarification to use a much larger band for illustration purposes, since this maneuver is one in which the ranks follow a repetitive action.

The actions and footwork necessary to form the company front are as follows:

1. The unit is marching in block formation.

2. The drum major orders the unit to close interval at the appropriate location.

3. After the unit comes to close interval it is in a configuration that allows the drum major to give the company front maneuver signal. After the signal of execution the drum major must position himself for the company front. He has many routes he can select to accomplish this. See *Diagram 42a.*

4. On the signal of execution the H rank (the last rank) stops its forward movement and, pivoting on H1, swings to the right 90 degrees as the spoke of a wheel. Note *Diagram 42a.*

5. The G rank takes two paces forward after the command of execution, then stops its forward movement and, pivoting on G1, swings to the right 90 degrees. Between H1 and G1 there are four full paces and five musicians must go into this space (H2, H3, H4, H5, and H6).

Diagram 42a / **The company front: phase one**

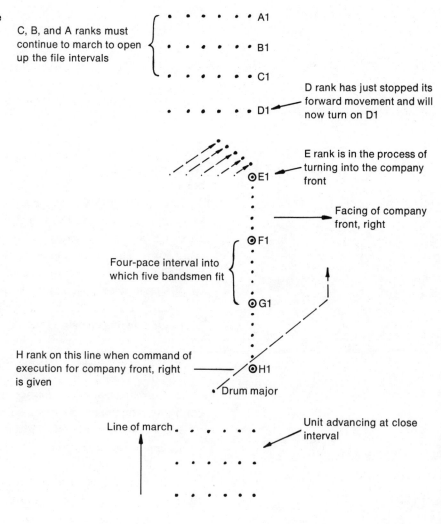

C, B, and A ranks must continue to march to open up the file intervals

A1

B1

C1

D rank has just stopped its forward movement and will now turn on D1

D1

E rank is in the process of turning into the company front

⊙E1

Facing of company front, right

⊙F1

Four-pace interval into which five bandsmen fit

⊙G1

H rank on this line when command of execution for company front, right is given

⊙H1

•Drum major

Line of march

Unit advancing at close interval

6. The F rank continues four paces forward after the command of execution is given, then, pivoting on F1, swings 90 degrees right, and so on through the remaining ranks. After the command of execution is given for the company front the A rank of the band continues forward for fourteen paces before pivoting on A1 to form the last element of the front. By this method the company front is formed from the back to the front. Each rank stays intact. The back to front formation necessitates some counting on the part of the bandsmen but there are numerous ways to accomplish this.

7. When the A rank turns into the line the company front is formed and all members of the band are marking time. The drum major can halt the men and the director can conduct an appropriate selection. See *Diagram 42a*.

NOTES ON FORMING THE COMPANY FRONT:

1. This company front can be formed without first going into the close interval formation; however, it is not quite as precise. It is executed in this manner: With the unit marching in block formation the drum major signals for a company front, right. The H rank halts its forward movement and, pivoting on H1, swings to the right 90 degrees. While the H rank swings into line it must close up in order to fit the five men into the four-pace interval allotted them in the company front line between G1 and H1. This sequence continues until the A rank has taken fourteen paces forward and made its pivot on A1.

2. Since each section of the company front is formed from the rear to the front, a definite count must be maintained by each rank to locate its turn line. It is not necessary for all six men in each rank to count the number of steps they take to their turning line. The men in the stem of the T, file number three, in this forty-eight-man block, can do the counting. They signal the time for their rank to turn into the company front line.

3. The drum major must be observant in order to center the formation correctly, because the positioning of the company front is determined by the position of the rear rank when the command of execution is given.

4. As the men complete their turns they should guide hard right on the number one men. They continue to mark time and align themselves. Once they face front, they should not attempt to realign themselves or they will cause the company front to whip.

5. The mark time can be halted by the drum major and the band turned over to the director for his selected music.

6. It is a good trick to make maneuvers look complicated or involved and yet have each man's movement rather elementary. This maneuver gives that impression. Orienting the unit by saying that it is marching due north, the company front can be formed facing east or west. It can be a company front, right, if it faces east or a company front, left, if it faces west. If the company front is to be formed facing east, the baton command means company front, right. If it is to be formed facing west, the baton command means company front, left. The bands-

men must know beforehand whether they will execute a company front, left, or a company front, right.

7. When the company front, right, is understood, the company front, left, becomes merely a process of reorientation.

The actions and footwork necessary to break the company front and reform the block are as follows:

1. The director turns command of the unit back to the drum major.

2. The drum major orders the reform sequence that will end in the block formation.

3. Each rank (rank of the block formation)in the company front pivots on its number one man. It turns clockwise 180 degrees as a wheel spoke until the company front is facing the opposite direction. This will require sixteen steps for a six-man rank. This is phase two, *Diagram 42b*. After the A rank turns the 180 degrees, it occupies the space previously held by the B rank, and so on for all ranks except H, which turns into a space not previously occupied.

Diagram 42b / **The company front: phase two**

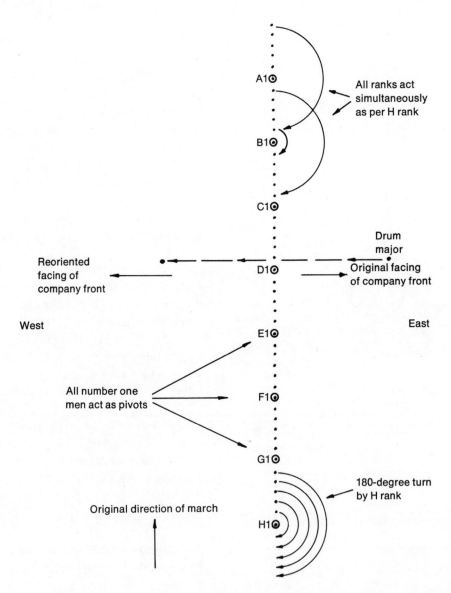

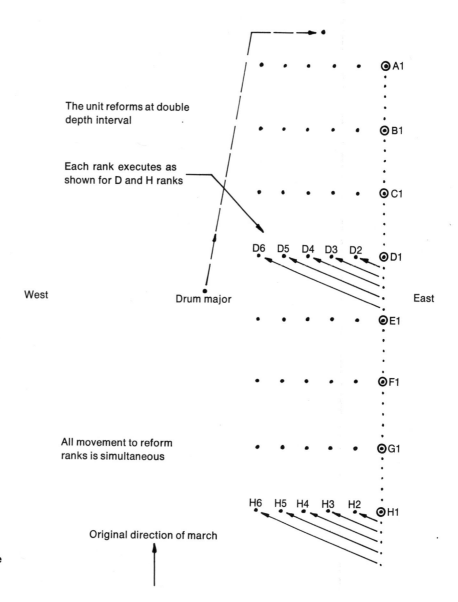

The unit reforms at double depth interval

Each rank executes as shown for D and H ranks

West

Drum major

East

D6 D5 D4 D3 D2 D1

All movement to reform ranks is simultaneous

H6 H5 H4 H3 H2 H1

Original direction of march

Diagram 43a / **The company front: phase three**

4. Upon a music cue or baton signal, the ranks in the reoriented company front move out at various angles to form an elongated block with a four-pace interval between ranks. The men mark time after forming the long block. This is phase three, *Diagram 43a*.

5. The regular block formation is reformed from the back to the front of the unit in the following manner:

a. On the "Forward—March" signal, the H rank steps off; the G rank marks time two steps, then steps off; the F rank marks time four steps, then steps off, and so on. This sequence is continued until the A rank marks time fourteen steps and steps off. At this point the block is reformed and moving on its original line of march. This is phase four, *Diagram 43b*.

b. Here again, not all men in each line need count steps; the guide man in each rank can count and signal "Forward."

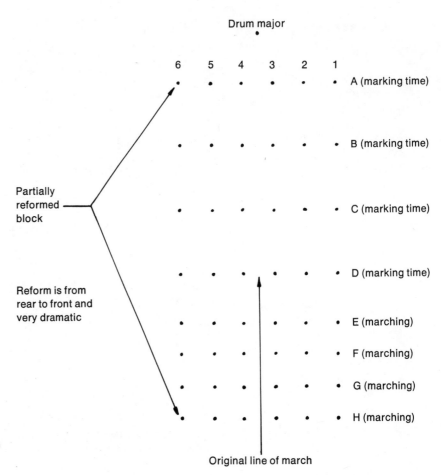

Drum major

6   5   4   3   2   1

•   •   •   •   •   •   A (marking time)

•   •   •   •   •   •   B (marking time)

Partially
reformed ——   •   •   •   •   •   •   C (marking time)
block

•   •   •   •   •   •   D (marking time)

Reform is from
rear to front and   •   •   •   •   •   •   E (marching)
very dramatic

•   •   •   •   •   •   F (marching)

•   •   •   •   •   •   G (marching)

•   •   •   •   •   •   H (marching)

Original line of march

Diagram 43b / **The company front: phase
four**

NOTES ON REFORMING THE BLOCK FORMATION FROM THE COMPANY FRONT:

1. An alternative to the preceding method of reforming the block is
to have the A rank step off on the forward march signal at a half step.
All other ranks step off with a full step. This is maintained until each
rank closes to its established file interval, at which time it assumes a
half step. No counting is necessary, but this method of reforming does
not have the eye appeal of the one illustrated in *Diagram 43b*.

2. The ranks pivoting on their number one man swing 180 degrees
as wheel spokes. They should be straight and remain intact while
turning.

3. The number one men, as the hubs of the spokes, pivot 180 degrees
on the spot on which they stand.

4. The number six men, who must travel the greatest distance in the
180-degree turn, should travel in their arc at a full step. The number
six men take the largest step. The number two men take the smallest
step.

5. The guide man for each rank in the 180-degree turn is the number six man, who takes a full pace during the turn.

6. When the men complete the 180-degree turn by ranks they are
in a second company front facing the audience that was at their backs.
The guide for this second company front is to the left. No corrective

alignment is necessary if the number one men do not drift while pivoting.

7. It is possible, with this type of reform, to center the company front in the middle of the field, salute one set of stands, execute the 180-degree turn by ranks, and have a second company front face the opposite set of stands.

General comments on the company front

1. The number of ways in which company fronts can be formed and the block reformed are almost limitless. The main objective of a particular design should be to fit it to the needs of the organization that will use it. Very few formations or maneuvers can be copied exactly. They must be modified for the organization that will use them. The important thing is to master design techniques and procedures. All else then becomes relatively simple.

2. The entire company front maneuver can be timed and cued with the music, with no drum major signal required, except the first one.

3. It is unfortunate that the description of the company front procedure must be more formidable than its actual performance.

Caution

None of the maneuvers in this entire chapter were designed for *your* band or corps. They are discussed in detail to illustrate techniques and procedures that you can use in designing maneuvers for your own organization.

**COLLEGE AND
HIGH SCHOOL BANDS**

Our school bands are unique. No other country in the world can boast of such an abundance of marching musical units composed of school-age musicians. They have become so much a part of our life that both the opening and half-time ceremonies of a football game without bands would be very dull indeed. When a parade is planned, the most important element for consideration is the number of marching musical units that can be obtained for the event; and our school bands are the main-stays of these parades. The American school bands add a great deal of tangible and intangible wealth to their schools and communities. In addition, the members of the bands have an opportunity, under proper leadership, to gain experience that will assist them throughout their lives, no matter what field of endeavor they may choose to follow.

For example, in band work the members are exposed to:

1. *Discipline.* The members of a school band are continually subjected to the discipline that is basic to every type of team effort.

2. *Cooperation.* Each member must cooperate with every other member of the group in order to produce the music and field work that, collectively, make a good band.

3. *Fellowship.* Friendships are formed that often result in life-long ties.

4. *Assurance.* Self-assurance is gained because the members are exposed to vast audiences during band performances.

Since the management of a marching musical unit is such a multi-sided endeavor having many inherent difficulties, a great number of areas always exist that should be subject to a continual evaluation. The following ideas and constructive criticisms have been selected from many discussed with the author by directors and bandsmen:

1. Football game activities for the band:

a. The initial entrance of the football team. The director, by ascertaining when the team will make its initial entry, can bring into play a rehearsed welcome formation. An aisle of bandsmen can be formed through which the team must pass in order to enter the field. The block formation must be moved into the correct location and broken into two single lines with the bandsmen facing each other. The band can play the school "fight song" as the team runs between the lines. After the team is on the field, the band should be reformed and marched to its seating section or held in readiness to play the National Anthem. See *Diagram 44.*

b. Music played by the band during the game. A problem of fully coordinating the music begins the moment that the unit is seated. The main difficulty seems to be that many members have such an interest in the game that they do not know which number is to be played next. This problem can be lessened, if not completely eliminated, by using large cards bearing the designated numbers of the required music and displaying them on an easel beside the director, facing the musicians. This gives the members a constant reference as to the next number to be played. In the event of a touchdown, the number displayed is disregarded, as everyone knows the tune of triumph. In addition to the problem just stated it frequently happens that both school bands will simultaneously begin playing at a time-out period. This is poor taste and can be corrected if the directors meet before the beginning of the activities and agree that each band will play alternately during the time-outs regardless of which team is ahead in the scoring. This is good sportsmanship.

c. The half-time show. The unit's big show at a football game is its half-time performance. It can be effectively improved as follows:

(1) A running commentary over the public address system during the band performance brings the audience in closer contact. The director should obtain the services of a special announcer for the band, one who is interested in its success and merits. An interested faculty member or student with a good voice can always be found who will take such an assignment and make it into a worthwhile project.

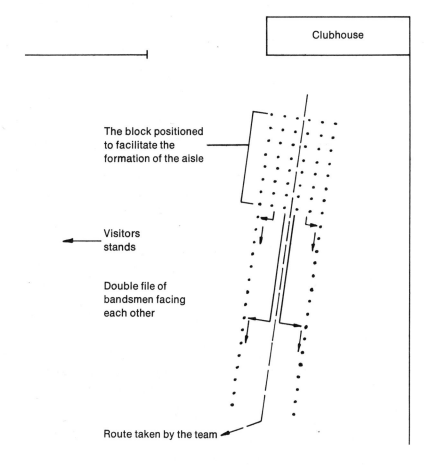

Diagram 44 / **Team entrance** Note: 1. After the aisle is formed the bandsmen continue to mark time. On signal they turn inward and halt. 2. After the passage of the team the band is reformed by reversing their entry routes.

Clubhouse

The block positioned to facilitate the formation of the aisle

Visitors stands

Double file of bandsmen facing each other

Route taken by the team

This announcer should work with the director and the band. He should be thoroughly familiar with the routine of the show and should conduct enough research to tie in some interesting sideline facts. The use of the public address system by the band announcer can be arranged by the school officials. A fact sheet about the band's performance should never be given cold to a disinterested announcer, whether or not he is a professional.

(2) The use of allotted radio and/or television half-time for interviewing some old football player who, with the announcer, runs down the plays that made up the first half of the game is considered by many to be an insult to both listening public and the band. This can be corrected. It must begin with pressure that can be exerted from the bands and the band leaders. The school boards must be informed of the situation and the radio and television officials should be briefed. It will require a minor crusade, but once the wishes of the audience are made known, the airways will carry the half-time show as readily as the football game.

(3) Another distraction that should be corrected is the interference from school groups, within the stadium itself, during the band's performance. The bandsmen put hundreds of man-hours into a show that lasts approximately seven minutes. One would think that this seven minutes would belong exclusively to the band. In many cases, while the band is working its heart out on its show, the cheerleader is screaming over a powerful PA system to a section of students, ordering the formation of some figure with colored cards or capes. The student demonstration section can be very effective and successful when used at the proper time. The proper time is not during the band's performance. Common courtesy should dictate this. Many times during the game there are time-outs called for one reason or the other, and these are actually dull moments as far as the audience is concerned. The bands play but there is nothing in particular to watch. Then is the time for the student demonstration section to form their figures. From a visual standpoint they will be the center of attention and their efforts can be fully appreciated.

d. After the game. This is a very difficult phase of a band's football game activities. A procedure that can be used at the end of the game that will ease the difficulty follows: As soon as the gun sounds the termination of the game, the band can file out of its seating area and form on the football field, facing the exit it will use. It does no harm to play one or two numbers while assembled on the field in block formation. This helps to add a finishing touch to the day's activities. If the band's own team has won the game, the victory song should certainly be played and, by the same token, if the opposing team has won the game, the band should play its school song. Following this presentation, the unit should leave the stadium playing a good march and finally be dismissed in an appointed area outside the stadium. The directors should check with each other so that both the music and march out can be coordinated.

e. The seating section reserved for the band. Stadium seating arrangements have been discussed at length by both musicians and

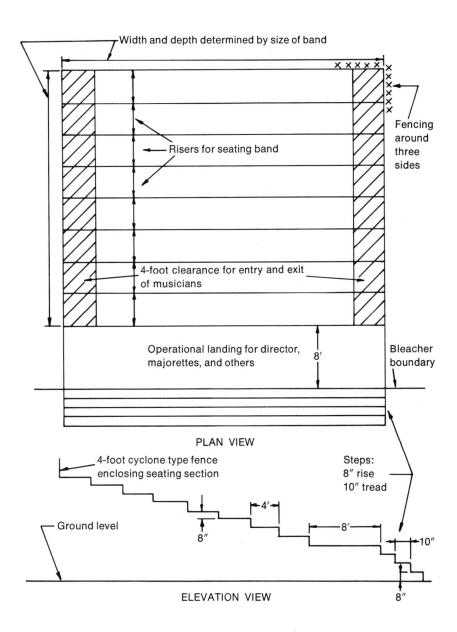

Width and depth determined by size of band

x x x x x

Fencing
around
three
sides

Risers for seating band

4-foot clearance for entry and exit
of musicians

Operational landing for director,
majorettes, and others

8'

Bleacher
boundary

PLAN VIEW

4-foot cyclone type fence
enclosing seating section

Steps:
8" rise
10" tread

Ground level

4'

8"

8'

10"

Diagram 45 / **Stadium seating**

ELEVATION VIEW

8"

8"

their directors. Seats are usually designed for the audience and are very inadequate for the band. Band members are usually seated on temporary bleachers much too narrow; or they are seated on folding chairs at ground level; or they are crowded into a small seating section of the stadium itself. Under none of these conditions can maximum performance proficiency be obtained. The band warrants a seating section especially designed to fit its needs:

(1) It should be located on the fifty-yard line. (The band deserves the best seats in the stadium.)

(2) It should be designed and built for the band. The landings should be four feet in depth and have a rise of about eight inches; the overall width and depth will be determined by the size of the unit.

(3) The seating area itself should contain a set of four-foot-wide stairs flanking each side to serve as passages for the musicians.

(4) The seats should be movable chairs with backs instead

of bleacher benches in order that they can be shifted or angled to meet the requirements of each musician.

(5) The band area should be closed to the surrounding audience and have a flight of steps leading to the stadium level. These steps should be as wide as the entire seating section. An eight-foot-wide landing running the entire width of the seating section should be located at the top of the steps, just in front of the tiered seating area. This landing is reserved for the director, majorettes, color guard, etc.

Such a seating section would add to the proficiency and prestige of the unit. When one calculates the total man-hours spent by the band preparing for a stadium performance and its value in the festivities, it appears that properly designed seating is not only deserved but should be a basic requirement. See *Diagram 45*.

f. Majorettes. These girls can contribute much to the overall performance of a marching musical unit whether they be two or twelve in number. They should consider themselves members of a team. They should rehearse intensely and work out movements coordinated with the music. It is not even essential that they twirl their batons; if they merely maintain a straight line and prance down the march line it will add an interesting feature to the show. With proper training and rehearsing they can easily master a dozen simple but coordinated movements and tricks that would really justify their existence and be a real asset to the organization.

If there are two or more majorettes, one should be in charge of the group. The one in charge should have a series of signals to effect coordinated response, just as the drum major has a special signal when he wishes the band to execute a maneuver. Here is a wide-open field for the majorettes to explore the use of definite signals to activate and sustain coordinated movement.

2. Working environment:

a. The rehearsal studio, practice area, supply room, and all inside areas connected with the operation of the unit should be so dressed and maintained that they have an atmosphere denoting efficiency and warmness.

(1) The rehearsal studio. This room should be systematically sized and arranged for optimum functional usage and should boast the following assets:

(a) Good lighting, which is absolutely essential.

(b) Good ventilation, which is also essential to good work.

(c) A section of blackboards that can be used for skull sessions.

(d) A screen on which slides and movies can be projected.

(e) A large bulletin board for schedules, commitments, and standard operating procedures.

(f) Acoustic damping to facilitate each musician's hearing his part and the parts played by the other members.

(g) A decor that denotes taste and care and also affords a friendly and cheerful atmosphere.

(2) Supply and repair. The supply and repair function is a very vital element in the overall operation. This segment of band activity should include the following:

(a) The supply and repair man should be a nonplaying member who will maintain all of the necessary records, make repairs, handle storage requirements, and arrange instrument transportation. (This is a full-time job.)

(b) The supply room should be of a proper size. A seventy-two-piece band requires a supply and repair room having a minimum of 500 square feet.

(c) The room should be off limits to all personnel except supply people and several key individuals approved by the director.

(d) A supply emergency kit is of the utmost importance. It should be carried on all of the unit's assignments. A suitcase, trap box, or fiber case can serve as a good emergency supply kit. This kit should contain such items as:

(1) Reeds and mouthpieces.

(2) Valve oil and lip ice.

(3) Mounted snare and batter heads, carried in a head retainer.

(4) One snare and one bass drum sling.

(5) Four snare drum sticks and a bass drum beater.

(6) Instrument repair tools.

(7) A first aid kit.

(8) A sewing kit with extra buttons, etc.

(9) Any other items deemed necessary to sustain the operation of the unit when it is away from its permanent supply room and studio.

b. Records: the band should maintain essential records such as:

(1) A detailed history of the organization, containing data on every practice, performance, and trip. This should be kept current at all times. To perform this task, one interested member of the unit should be selected as historian.

(2) A scrapbook should be maintained to keep all clippings on the unit's activities.

(3) There should be a publicity man, who can be a member of the unit. He should make a project of working with the newspapers to publicize the organization. He should have a prepared document on the band to distribute to out-of-town news media whenever the unit is traveling.

(4) The "director's control board" should be a large plywood board neatly painted and fitted with small hooks on which can be hung circular tags carrying the position designations, instrumentation, and names of the members. The board should also contain other facets of the unit's overall operation such as the special drum unit, majorettes, and utility members. Such a board keeps the director informed, at all times, of the status of his organization. The task of keeping the board current can be assigned to an interested member or the director may wish to handle it himself. See *Diagram 46.*

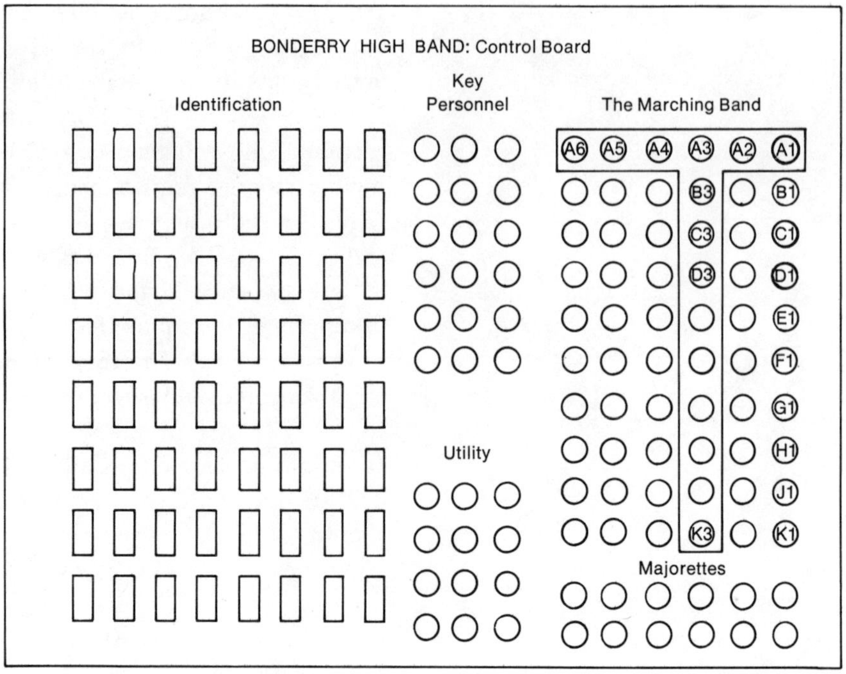

BONDERRY HIGH BAND: Control Board

Identification   Key Personnel   The Marching Band

A6 A5 A4 A3 A2 A1
B3 B1
C3 C1
D3 D1
E1
F1
G1

Utility   H1
J1
K3 K1

Majorettes

Diagram 46 / **Director's control board**

Every band and drum corps should have a glee club or "sing along" activity. This does not imply that the marching band should have an accomplished glee club of ten or twenty voices. The vocalizing does not have to be polished in a musical sense, because it is not intended that it be presented to an audience. Actually, little time need be spent on the glee club project other than to pass out mimeographed copies of the words to ten good songs and to hold short rehearsals at appropriate moments. On a bus, train, or in a dressing room these songs will be sung spontaneously without direction or supervision. There are times when the singing will ease tensions and build morale.

The foregoing projects are not self-starting. They require work, diplomacy, and patience on the part of everyone concerned. Once the members of the unit start these projects, the band will become a much more personal part of their lives. Speed is not all-important; a plan of never-ending improvement is the key. This means that extra thought and activity will be required of the director and other key personnel, but the dividends are far-reaching. Once it has been proved to the sponsors that the unit has a program of self-improvement there is less difficulty obtaining the necessary funds.

DRUM AND BUGLE CORPS The drum and bugle corps capitalizes on showmanship, flashy march routines, and tricky musical arrangements. While this entire book pertains to the drum and bugle corps just as it does to bands, there are some special operational facets that are peculiar to the corps. After witnessing several dozen corps competitions I feel that a number of constructive criticisms can be offered for consideration:

1. In corps competitions, the wheeling, maneuvering, and footwork have good audience appeal up to a certain point, but past this point they become repetitious. Drum corps that do compete might review the advantages of devoting part of their time on the field to a big production number. During half of the allotted performance time the unit could "strut its stuff" with rapid precision movements. During the remaining half of the time a production number, with a libretto or story background, could be staged. The field from which to choose a theme for a production number is unlimited.

a. A salute to the air industry with appropriate music and formations to complement the occasion.

b. A salute to the American Legion with suitable music and formations to fit the occasion, or in the same vein, the VFW.

c. Production number of American dances with accompanying steps and music.

d. A salute to the United Nations.

e. A salute to the American Indian.

The production type of number gives the audience an opportunity to witness a sustained and meaningful story.

2. Much of the time in competitive performances the unit is playing to a fence or the empty side of the stadium. Field maneuvers should be flexible enough to have the entire show face the audience if the audience is grouped on one side of the field. If the audience is located on both sides of the field, the show should then be performed accordingly. The performers should play to the audience at all times.

3. When the unit is on parade, a baton is an absolute necessity. A baton does nothing more than lengthen the arm of the man who is giving orders. It assists the drum major to obtain coordinated and timely response. A unit appears polished and well trained if it executes commands together. Some directors prefer a whistle to a baton, but it would require an elaborate series of coded signals on a whistle to accomplish what the baton can do with ease. (In addition, whistles remind people of a situation that is out of control.)

4. The closing ceremonies of a drum corps competition are among the most spectacular field shows that can be seen anywhere. There are literally thousands of important items to be correlated and therefore many opportunities exist to make procedural errors. Here are some suggestions that may assist in clearing up some of the gray areas of the competition finale:

a. The lineup—positioning the units in "a mass front" on a predetermined line. This is the beginning of the formal final ceremony, after the individual acts have been completed by the competing corps.

(1) The director of each unit orders his group onto the line.

(2) The first unit to be placed on the line should be the host corps, which will play "Sound Off," "Retreat," and "To the Colors." This organization proceeds to the number one position on the right side of the line. After it is in place, the other corps may be marched to the line, one at a time.

(3) The approach to the predetermined line from the assembly area should be a straight route, as indicated in *Diagram 47*.

(4) A unit may approach the line on a drum tap or with music, but as soon as it is on line the cadence or music must be cut. The director then orders, "Parade—Rest." He then faces front and assumes parade rest.

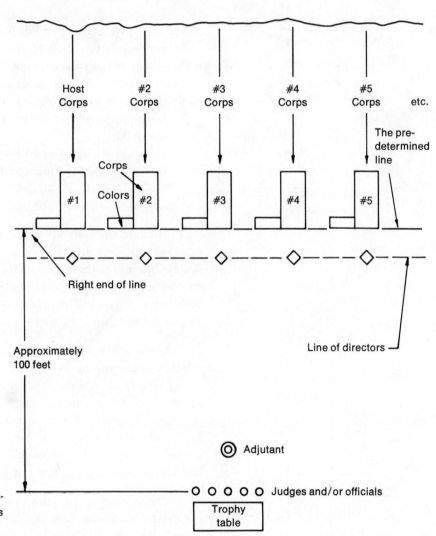

Diagram 47 / **The lineup** All corps assemble in this area as individual units with their colors.

(5) The color team marches to the line with its corps and positions itself on the right of the corps.

(6) When all of the participating units are on the line and at parade rest, the adjutant commands, "Report." Beginning at the right, the director of each unit comes to attention and reports, "Green Corps —Present, Sir," and so on down the line, one at a time, from right to left. After a unit director reports, he again assumes the position of parade rest. Note Diagram 47.

b. The sound off and trooping of the line by the host corps.

(1) Immediately after the report is taken, the adjutant commands, "Sound off." On the adjutant's command the director of the

number one corps comes to attention, does an about-face, calls his unit to attention, commands, "Sound off," then directs the sound off, which consists of three specified chords.

(2) After the three chords are played, the corps immediately steps off to music, makes a left turn, troops to the end of the line, executes a box reverse and returns to its original position by the same route.

(3) When the unit is back on the line, oriented as it was when it sounded the first three chords, the music is cut and immediately the same three chords are sounded. This is the complete sound off routine.

(4) During the sound off all colors and all other corps remain at parade rest on the line.

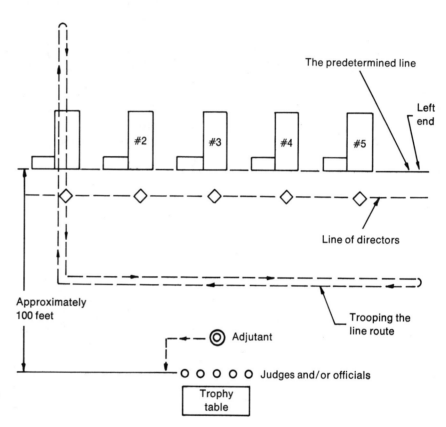

Diagram 48 / **Sound off and trooping the line**

(5) It is also correct to execute sound off in place in the following manner. The adjutant commands, "Sound off in place." The director then merely has the unit sound the three chords; that is all, no more music, no movement. This is used when it is desired to cut down the time of the finale. See *Diagram 48.*

c. The presentation of awards.

(1) After the final three chords of the sound off are played the directors come to attention. The adjutant orders, "Directors, front and center—March." All directors (one for each corps) participate in this. If they are to the left of the adjutant as they face him, they execute a right face and march toward the center of the line of directors.

If they are to the right of the adjutant as they face him, they execute left face and march toward the center of the line of directors.

(2) The left and right groups converge until the spaces between the directors are about thirty inches. They then turn front and step off together toward the adjutant. The director of the host corps gives all movement commands once they converge at the thirty-inch interval on the route to the adjutant. The directors halt six feet from the adjutant.

(3) The adjutant executes an about-face and reports to the chief official, "Sir, the persons to be awarded are present." The adjutant then moves to one side.

(4) As the appointed official announces the awards, the director who is to receive the award takes one pace forward, halts, and salutes. The official salutes and presents the award. Any movement necessary to present the award is done by the awarding official; the receiver takes only one pace forward. Following the presentation of the award, the director takes one pace backward into the line of directors and holds at attention. Each director who receives an award follows this procedure.

(5) After all of the awards are presented, the directors execute an about-face on an order from the director of the host corps and retrace the routes to their units. After the awards are presented the sequence of voice command is "About—Face; Forward—March; Di-

Diagram 49 / **Directors front and center** (Presentation of Awards)

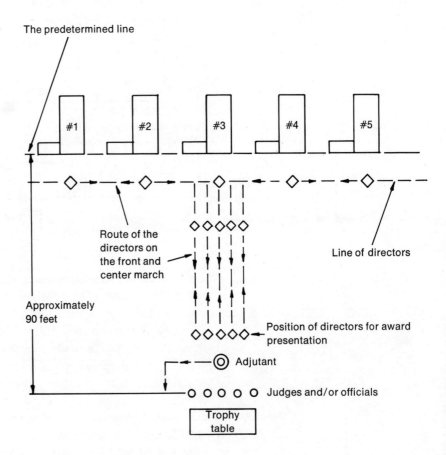

rectors—Halt; Outward—Face." (Here the commanders face the direction in which they must proceed to return to their units.) The final voice command is "Forward—March." The directors proceed to their positions, halt and face front. This sequence of commands can be followed by observing *Diagram 49.*

d. Retreat and to the colors.

The retreat exercise is the most solemn part of the ceremony. This is the point where the contestants and audience pay their respect and allegiance to our flag and country.

(1) As soon as the directors are repositioned in front of their respective units following the award presentation, the adjutant commands, "Sound retreat." All units and personnel hold at parade rest with the exception of the number one (host) corps.

(2) The director of the number one corps snaps to attention; executes about-face; calls his unit to attention, and directs the retreat music.

(3) Immediately upon completion of this music, the other directors come to the position of attention, execute about-face, individually call their corps to attention, and order, "Present arms." (The musicians hold at attention.) The unit directors then execute about-face and render a hand salute.

(4) The number one unit plays "To the Colors."

(5) When this music is ended, the directors drop their salutes, execute about-face, and command their units, "Order arms." The directors execute about-face.

e. Pass in review and exit.

(1) At the completion of the music "To the Colors," the adjutant executes about-face and reports to the head official, "Sir, the parade is formed." The official replies, "Have it pass in review."

(2) The adjutant commands, "Pass in review" and then resumes the same position he held when the awards were presented.

(3) The number one corps steps off with music, makes a left turn, and passes in review. As the number one corps makes its left turn, the second unit makes a right turn silently and then a left, and holds at the position designated in *Diagram 50.* The first unit continues its music until it passes a designated point on the line of march. The director then cuts the music and marches his unit to a location where it can be dismissed.

(4) As soon as the first corps stops playing, the second steps off with music. The prepositioning maneuver described for the second unit is emulated in turn by each succeeding corps from right to left down the line of corps.

(5) The route for the pass in review is the same for all units. Since each of the corps must start the pass in review from the right end of the line, two extra turns and some movement are necessary to reach the starting position.

(6) After all units have passed in review, the colors are dismissed and finally the musicians are dismissed.

(7) In the pass in review each color team is in front of its

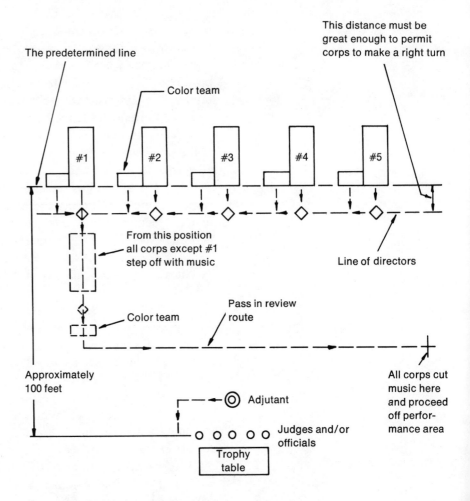

The predetermined line

This distance must be great enough to permit corps to make a right turn

Color team

#1 #2 #3 #4 #5

From this position all corps except #1 step off with music

Line of directors

Color team

Pass in review route

Approximately 100 feet

All corps cut music here and proceed off performance area

Adjutant

Judges and/or officials

Trophy table

Diagram 50 / **Pass in review**

corps. The color teams assume this position before the corps steps off from its line position to the starting position.

(8) All corps directors and color teams, except the national emblem, salute as they pass the judges and officials.

COLOR TEAMS A color team normally consists of one national emblem, one state flag, one Legion or VFW flag, two color guards, and a color team commander. The color guard is the protector of the emblem; therefore, this section will refer to color guards when speaking of the guards, flag bearers when speaking of the emblem carriers, and color team when speaking of the entire group. The composition of a color team is flexible and can be cut down or augmented. There is no set formula for combinations. From the standpoint of visual balance it is much better if all ensigns are the same size and all the carrying staffs are the same length. No secondary flag should be larger than the national emblem or on a longer staff. See *Diagram 51.*

No rules are more exactly written than are those concerning the use of our country's flag. There are several good booklets on the use of our national colors. Pamphlets may be obtained from:

1. The US Government Printing Office, Washington, D.C. (Request Public Law 829 of the Seventy-Seventh Congress, Second Session.)

2. The US Naval Recruiting Service has an excellent folder on the use of the flag.

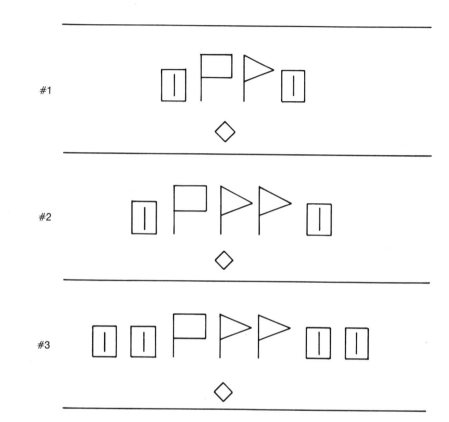

Diagram 51 / **Color team combinations**

KEY:

◇ Commander

⊐ National emblem

▷ Miscellaneous flag or banner

▯ Color guard

There are many operational and performance situations that confront a color team working with a corps or band; however, they can be grouped into five general areas:

1. Receiving the colors.

The colors must be formally received before they are used as part of the activities with a band or corps.

a. To receive the colors, the entire organization is assembled in block formation and the musicians are called to attention by the director or drum major. The color team commander orders, "Advance the colors—March." The color team advances to within ten feet in front of the musicians and halts facing the corps or band. The color team commander orders, "Present—Arms"; the marching musicians hold at attention; the color guards present arms; all flags except the national emblem are dipped; the commander, facing the colors, renders a hand salute and holds the salute for ten seconds; he then breaks the salute and commands, "Order—Arms"; all colors are raised.

b. The color team commander orders, "Left wheel—March," and the color team changes its facing 180 degrees. Color teams never use "To the Rear" or "About Face." See *Diagram 52.*

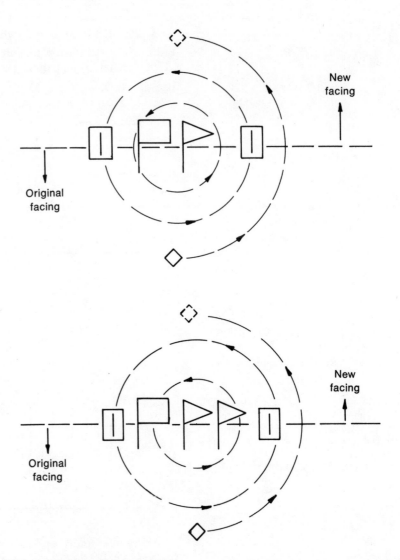

Diagram 52 / **The left wheel movement**
Two examples of the left wheel movement which turns the color team 180 degrees and emerges with the national emblem on the right of the other flags. Above, the right guard and national emblem turn in a forward direction, the other two turn by moving backward. The commander takes the route shown. Below, The center emblem bearer pivots 180 degrees in place, the right guard and national emblem turn in a forward direction, the other two turn by moving backward. The commander takes the route shown.

KEY:

⬚ Color guard

◇ Team commander

⌐ National emblem

▷ Other flag

c. The entire organization is now ready to move or be given "Rest" or "At Ease" until the event begins.

NOTE: The colors should never be received until a few minutes before the scheduled event begins.

2. Parades.

a. In each parade there is either a reviewing stand or designated official point the colors must pass. The passage of this point should be conducted as follows: Five paces from the stand, the color team commander orders, "Eyes—Right" (or "Left" as required). Supposing the reviewing stand is on the right, where it should be if correctly located, at the command "Eyes—Right" the following should occur simultaneously:

(1) The color team commander does "Eyes Right" and renders a hand salute.

(2) The color guard on the right keeps head and eyes to the front and renders a rifle salute.

(3) The color guard on the left does "Eyes Right" and renders a rifle salute.

(4) The national emblem bearer does "Eyes Right" and holds the flag erect.

(5) The other flag bearers do "Eyes Right" and lower their flags.

b. When the color team is five paces past the reviewing stand, the commander orders, "Ready—Front," at which time all eyes turn front, salutes are broken, and the colors come back up. There is no hesitation in the march. This is a very simple but inspiring performance.

3. Corps competitions.

The most interesting event for the corps color team is the corps competition. In the course of the competition the color team must present its competitive offering and several other special activities.

a. Receiving the colors.

(1) The colors must be received by the assembled corps. "Receiving the Colors" has already been described, but with a little additional planning, it can be made even more effective by receiving the colors en masse. A massed colors ceremony must be arranged in advance by the host corps.

(a) Before the competition begins, all color teams should be assembled on the opposite side of the field from the officials' stand. The colors should be uncased and a mass color team formed. The front rank of the team must be composed of national emblems, flanked on each side by one color guard. The second rank, six feet back, should be made up of state and other flags, which can be grouped according to their corps. The third rank, six feet back of the second rank, can be composed of color guards. The mass color team commander should be stationed six feet in front of the first rank.

(b) The color team commander next calls the mass color team to attention and orders, "Forward—March." A single drum tap should be used to keep cadence. The unit proceeds across the field until the commander is ten feet from the assembled officials, at which time he commands, "Color Team—Halt." The mass team halts and the color team commander executes an about-face and orders, "Present—Arms." The commander salutes for ten seconds; the national colors remain erect and all other flags are dipped. The color guards present arms (use a rifle salute). The officials give a hand salute. The audience should stand and render a civilian salute. After ten seconds, the color team commander orders, "Order—Arms."

(c) To remove the mass team from the field, the national colors must lead. The color team commander orders, "Right—Face," and "Column of files from the left, forward—March." The national flags, flanked by the two guards, step off; the other flags and color guards mark time. The head of the file of secondary flags follows in file as the last of the national colors pass. As the last member of the second file passes the head of the file of color guards, it follows in file. This makes one single file marching down the side line with a single drum tap for cadence.

(d) When the column of files is away from the receiving

area the commander orders, "Color team—Halt." The group halts and the commander orders, "Join your units."

(e) NOTE: If the massed color team is very large it would be wise to have each man march to a designated point, for example the zero yard line on the line of march. From that point each should proceed directly to his respective unit. Note *Diagram 53.*

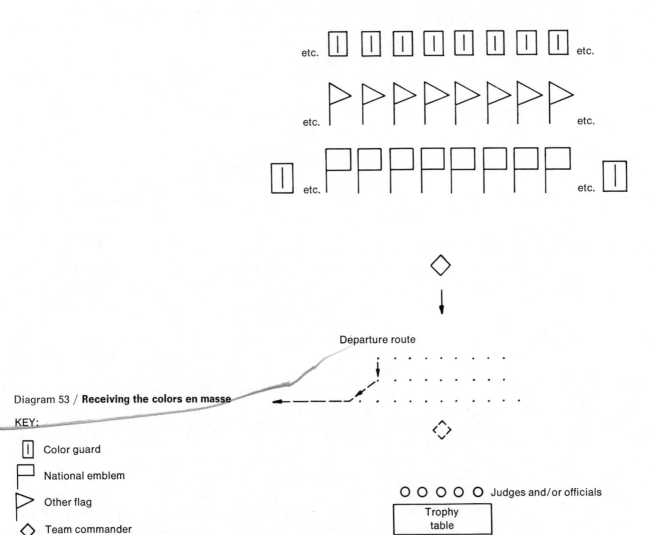

Diagram 53 / **Receiving the colors en masse**

KEY:

| Color guard

National emblem

Other flag

Team commander

Departure route

Judges and/or officials

Trophy table

b. Dismissing the colors.

The colors must be dismissed before the band or corps is dismissed at the end of the event. The entire organization (colors and musicians) is halted. The color team makes a left wheel movement in order to face the unit, which is at attention. The color team commander orders "Present—Arms," at which time all flags except the national emblem are lowered; the color guard presents arms; the commander, facing the flag, holds a salute for ten seconds, then breaks the salute and commands, "Order—Arms." All return to attention, and the order to dismiss is given. The national flag is immediately rolled up and cased.

c. The retreat ceremony.

(1) "To the Colors" is the field music for the national anthem. It can be used in lieu of "The Star-Spangled Banner" and it is the proper substitution for the national anthem. (Refer to the retreat exercise explained in the section "Drum and Bugle Corps.")

(2) If there is a flagpole on the field with a flag attached to it, the flag should be brought down during the rendition of "To the Colors" or "The Star-Spangled Banner," whichever is played. One color team or a group of veterans must be assigned the task of lowering the flag.

d. Pass in review.

The color team procedure for the pass in review has previously been explained.

e. Dismissing the colors.

After the pass in review the colors are dismissed by each corps as previously explained.

4. Flagpole ceremonies.

a. A color team should be well trained in the correct use of the flag for flagpole ceremonies. It sometimes happens that the team will be asked to handle the flag at the dedication of a building, airport, or similar occasion. The color team for a flagpole ceremony should be composed of five persons—one color team commander, two color guards, one flag bearer, and one helper. The helper assists in getting the flag up or down the pole as the situation requires and also assists in folding it. Usually the occasion calls for a flag-raising ceremony; should it call for a flag-lowering ceremony, the general procedure is still the same.

b. The color team is formed some distance away from the flag-pole. It is then marched to the flagpole and halted. The team commander orders parade rest. The team commander orders the unit to prepare to raise the flag. The color guards hold fast; the flag bearer and helper move to the flagpole. See *Diagram 54*.

c. If the flag is to be raised, the helper frees the ropes and then assists the flag bearer in attaching the folded flag to the snaps of the rope. Each man takes a rope and assumes parade rest. After retreat and just prior to the beginning of the national anthem or "To the Colors," the team commander orders "Attention" and "Present Arms." When the music begins, the men holding the ropes raise the flag rapidly and tie the ropes. They then step back and salute until the end of the music.

d. If the flag is to be lowered, the same position is taken. When the national anthem or "To the Colors" is begun, the men lower the flag slowly, timed so that they can grasp it as the music ends. The color team commander and guards are at present arms as the music is played. After the music ends, whether it be "The Star-Spangled Banner" or "To the Colors," the salute is broken.

e. The team is reformed facing the flag pole by the commander, who orders, "Fall in." (In a flag-lowering ceremony, the commander must give the two flag handlers time to fold the emblem before reforming the team.) The bearers fall in between the guards facing the flagpole.

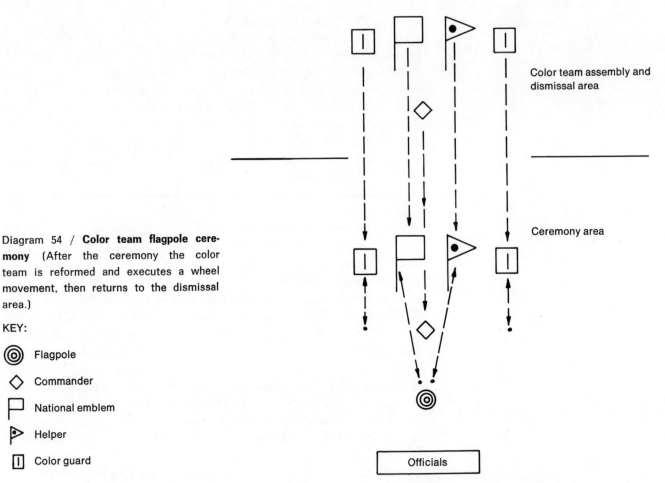

Color team assembly and dismissal area

Ceremony area

Officials

Diagram 54 / **Color team flagpole ceremony** (After the ceremony the color team is reformed and executes a wheel movement, then returns to the dismissal area.)

KEY:

◎ Flagpole

◇ Commander

⌂ National emblem

▷ Helper

⏛ Color guard

The commander orders, "Left wheel—March" and takes his position at the front of the group. Following the wheel movement the team members are all marking time. The commander orders, "Forward—March." They march to the assembly area, are halted, and dismissed. In addition to the color team's activities with their corps or band the members should be authorities on the rules and regulations governing the use of the national emblem. Each member of the color team should be well trained on the use of the colors for all circumstances. It is the color team commander's responsibility to train the team.

Various rules governing the use of the flag

1. The national emblem should always be to the right of any other flags carried by the color team. This is the reason a color team cannot execute "About Face" or "To the Rear" because either of these maneuvers would put the Stars and Stripes to the left of the other flags.

2. The left wheel movement which color teams perform to change their direction 180 degrees will always keep the national flag to the right of all others, this is its correction location. The wheel movement is quite simple and is shown in Diagram 52.

3. Turns are movements that must be used continually by color teams. A right or left, or half right or half left, turn is executed by a color team as a spoke movement, not as a flanking movement. When a 90-degree left turn must be made it is performed thusly: At the correct

time the color team commander gives "Left Turn—March," and on the command of execution the guard on the left marks time on the spot and rotates 90 degrees left; the other members turn with him as though he were the hub of a wheel and they formed the spoke. Once the group is around the turn and is marking time, the color team commander may give, "Forward—March." The right turn is executed in a similar manner.

4. The flags should be cased until they are to be received and cased again immediately upon dismissal. If the flags must be moved around by the bearers when not in official formation, they should be held tight against the staff.

5. Display and salute of the flag:

a. The flag of the United States represents the nation, the union (blue field and stars) being the honor point. The right is the place of honor. The edge that is toward the staff is the right edge. The union and the flag itself are always given the place of honor.

b. The United States flag, colors, or standard should never be dipped in salute, nor should it ever be permitted to touch the ground. The flag should never be used as a costume, dress, or drapery in any form, or on a vehicle or float except attached to a staff. For draping and decoration in general, bunting of the national colors may be used, with the blue uppermost. No lettering or object of any kind should be placed on the United States flag, nor should the flag be used in any form of advertising.

c. When displayed horizontally or vertically against a wall, the flag should be flat, with the union uppermost to the flag's own right (the observer's left).

d. When displayed over the middle of a street, the flag should be suspended vertically with the union to the north in an east-west street or to the east in a north-south street. The flag should be at such height as to clear all traffic. However, when suspended over a sidewalk on a pole extending from a building, the union should be toward the pole.

e. To indicate mourning, the flag is placed at half-staff. It is hoisted to the top of the staff before it is lowered to the half-staff position and hoisted again before it is lowered from the half-staff position. On Memorial Day, the flag is displayed at half-staff from sunrise (reveille) until noon and at full-staff from noon until sunset (retreat). When prescribed by regulations or specifically ordered by proper authority, colors and standards are draped to indicate mourning. Two streamers of black crepe seven feet long and about twelve inches wide are attached to the staff below the spearhead.

f. At a funeral, the flag is placed lengthwise on the casket with the union at the head and over the left shoulder of the deceased. The casket is carried foot first. The flag is not lowered into the grave.

g. In a procession with a line of other flags, the United States flag is in front of the center of the line. In a procession with a single other flag, the United States flag is on the marching right.

h. When the United States flag and those of other nations are flown from adjacent staffs, the United States flag should be at the right end of the line or to the observer's left. When flown with flags of other nations, all staffs should be of equal height and the flags of equal size insofar as possible. International usage forbids display of one national flag above that of another in time of peace. Where the United States flag is one of several flags flown on adjacent staffs, it will be hoisted first and lowered last. In a group of flags of states, cities, or societies, all displayed from staffs, the United States flag should be at the center of and at the highest point in the group.

i. When displayed with another flag from crossed staffs against a wall, the United States flag will be on the right (the left of the observer facing the wall), and its staff will be in front of that of the other flag.

j. In a chapel, if displayed within the chancel, the United States flag is at the chaplain's right as he faces the congregation, and other flags at his left. If displayed in front of the chancel, the United States flag is on the right of the congregation as they face the chaplain, and other flags are on the congregation's left. Similarly, at an assembly where there is a speaker's platform, indoors or outdoors, the United States flag is at the right of the speaker's stand if on the platform and at the right of the audience if not on the platform. Other flags should be located on the side opposite from the national emblem. If the United States flag is displayed against the wall behind the speaker, it should be above and behind the speaker's stand.

k. On an automobile or on a float in a parade, the flagstaff may be fastened to the bumper bracket or in such other upright position that the flag is displayed prominently and will not be soiled by drooping or blowing against the vehicle.

l. During the ceremony of hoisting or lowering the flag, or when it is passing in a parade or in a review, all persons present, except those actually engaged in hoisting or lowering the flag, should face it, stand at attention, and salute. Men who are not in uniform should remove their headdress with the right hand and hold it at the left shoulder, over the heart. Women should salute by placing the right hand over the heart. The salute to the flag in a moving column is rendered as the flag passes.

m. An unserviceable silk organizational national flag should not be destroyed but should be numbered and retained as a memento of service by the organization to which it belongs.

n. Soiled, torn, or badly faded non-organizational flags should not be displayed. They should be destroyed by burning privately.

o. Flags should never be rolled on the staff while wet or damp. They should be hung flat to dry.

Notes on the manual of arms for the color guard

1. The snap and zing of any color team lies for the most part in the training, proficiency, and pride of the color guard. The rifle carriers must master the manual of arms for their weapons.

a. In all positions of the left hand at the balance, the thumb clasps the rifle; the sling is included in the grasp of the hand. In describing the manual of arms, the term "at the balance" refers to points on rifles as follows:

(1) U. S. rifle, caliber .30 M1: a point just forward of the trigger housing.

(2) U. S. rifle, caliber .30 M1903: the center of the rear sight.

b. In all positions of the rifle, diagonally across the body, the barrel is up, butt in front of the right hip, barrel crossing opposite the junction of the neck with the left shoulder. The rifle is grasped at the balance with the left hand, palm toward the body, wrist straight. The cadence of the motions is that of quick time. Trainees are first required to give their whole attention to the details of the motions, the cadence being gradually acquired as they become accustomed to handling their rifles. The instructor may require them to count aloud in cadence with the motions. The manual is taught at a halt. For the purpose of instruction, it may be taught by the numbers. The manual is not executed in marching except when marching at attention. When marching at attention the rifle may be changed from the right shoulder to the left shoulder or to port arms and the reverse. These movements may be used to add interest to the drill or to prevent fatigue in long marches at attention. Any appropriate position of the manual of arms may be ordered from a previous position by giving the suitable commands.

c. Position of order arms: The butt of the rifle rests on the ground, barrel to the rear, toe of the butt on line with the toe and touching the right shoe, right hand holding the rifle between the thumb and fingers, left hand as in the position of at attention without arms.

d. Trail arms: Being at order arms, the command is "Trail—Arms." At the command "Arms," raise the rifle and incline the muzzle forward so that the barrel makes an angle of about 15 degrees with the vertical, the right arm slightly bent.

e. Order arms: Being at trail arms, the command is "Order—Arms." At the command "Arms," lower the rifle with the right hand.

f. Port arms: Being at order arms, the command is "Port—Arms." At the command "Arms," raise the rifle with the right hand and carry it diagonally across the front of the body until the right hand is in front of and slightly to the left of the face so that the barrel is up, butt in front of the right hip, barrel crossing opposite the junction of the neck and the left shoulder. At the same time, grasp the rifle at the balance with the left hand, palm toward the body, wrist straight. On the count of two, carry the right hand to the small of the stock, grasping it, palm down, holding right forearm horizontal; left elbow resting against the body; the rifle in a vertical plane parallel to the front.

g. Present arms: Being at order arms, the command is "Present—Arms." At the command "Arms," with the right hand carry the rifle in front of the center of the body, barrel to the rear and vertical; grasp it with the left hand at the balance, forearm horizontal and resting against the body. On the count of two, grasp the small of the stock with the right hand.

h. Order arms: Being at present arms or port arms, the command is "Order—Arms." At the command "Arms," move the right hand from its grasp of the stock and regrasp the rifle between the upper sling swivel and stacking swivel. On the count of two, release the grasp of the left hand and lower the rifle to the right so that the butt is three inches from the ground, barrel to the rear, left hand with fingers extended and joined, steadying the rifle, forearm and wrist straight and inclining downward. On the count of three complete the order by lowering the rifle gently to the ground with the right hand. Cut away the left hand smartly to the side. Care must be exercised to insure that the rifle is lowered gently and not thrust down forcibly.

i. Inspection arms: Being at order arms, the command is "Inspection—Arms."

(1) U.S. rifle, caliber .30 M1: At the command "Arms," take the position of port arms. On the count of three, with the fingers of the left hand closed, place the left thumb on the operating rod handle and push it smartly to the rear until it is caught off the operating rod catch; at the same time lower the head and eyes sufficiently to glance into the receiver. On the count of four, having found the magazine empty or having emptied it, raise the head and eyes to the front, at the same time regrasping the piece with the left hand at the balance.

(2) U.S. rifle, caliber, M1903: At the command "Arms," take the position of port arms. On the count of three, seize the bolt handle with the thumb and forefinger of the right hand, turn the handle up, draw the bolt back, and lower the head and eyes sufficiently to glance into the magazine. On the count of four, having found the magazine empty or having emptied it, raise the head and eyes to the front.

(3) Whatever preparatory command follows the inspection order, the bolt of the rifle is sent into closed position and the trigger is pulled. After pulling the trigger, immediately assume port arms. (This is all done on the preparatory command of the next movement.)

j. Right shoulder arms: Being at order arms, the command is "Right Shoulder—Arms." At the command "Arms," raise and carry the rifle diagonally across the body with the right hand, at the same time grasping it at the balance with the left hand. On the count of two, regrasp it with the right hand on the butt, the heel between the first two fingers, thumb and fingers closed on the stock. On the count of three, without changing the grasp of the right hand, place the rifle on the right shoulder, barrel up, and inclined at an angle of about 45 degrees from the horizontal, trigger guard in the hollow of the shoulder, right elbow against the side, forearm horizontal, the rifle in a vertical plane perpendicular to the front. Carry the left hand, thumb and fingers extended and joined, to the small of the stock, first joint of the forefinger touching the rear end of the receiver (or, for the M1903 rifle, the cocking piece), wrist straight, and elbow down. On the count of four, cut away the left hand smartly to the side.

k. Port arms: Being at right shoulder arms, the command is "Port—Arms." At the command "Arms," press the rifle butt down quickly and throw the rifle diagonally across the body, at the same time turning the butt clockwise one-quarter turn so as to bring the barrel up, the right hand retaining its grasp on the butt, the left grasping the rifle at the balance. On the count of two, change the right hand to the small of the stock.

l. Order arms: Being at right shoulder arms, the command is "Order—Arms." At the command "Arms," execute the first movement prescribed in paragraph k. for port arms from right shoulder arms. On the counts of two, three, and four, execute the last two movements prescribed in paragraph h. for order arms from port arms.

m. Right shoulder arms: Being at port arms, the command is "Right Shoulder—Arms." At the command "Arms," change the right hand to the butt as described in paragraph j. On the counts of two and three, execute the last two movements prescribed in paragraph j. for right shoulder arms from order arms.

n. Left shoulder arms: Being at port arms, the command is "Left Shoulder—Arms." At the command "Arms," release the grip of the left hand on the rifle, and with the right hand still grasping the small of the stock, place it on the left shoulder, barrel up, trigger guard in the hollow of the shoulder. At the same time, grasp the butt with the left hand, heel of the butt between the first and second fingers, thumb and fingers closed on the stock, left forearm horizontal, left elbow against the side, the rifle in a vertical plane perpendicular to the front. On the count of two, drop the right hand quickly to the right side. Left shoulder arms may be ordered when rifles are at the order, right shoulder, or present. At the command "Arms," execute port arms and continue in cadence to the position ordered.

o. Port arms: Being at left shoulder arms, the command is "Port —Arms." At the command "Arms," grasp the rifle with the right hand at the small of the stock. On the count of two, release the grasp of the left hand and at the same time carry the piece with the right hand to the position of port arms and then regrasp it with the left.

p. Right shoulder arms: Being at left shoulder arms, the command is "Right Shoulder—Arms." At the command "Arms," execute port arms as described in paragraph o. and continue in cadence to the position ordered as described in paragraph j.

q. Parade rest: Being at order arms, the command is "Parade— Rest." At the command "Rest," move the left foot smartly twelve inches to the left of the right foot, keeping the legs straight so that the weight of the body rests equally on both feet. At the same time incline the muzzle of the rifle to the front, the right arm extended, right hand grasping the rifle just below the upper band. Place and hold the left hand behind the body, resting in the small of the back, palm to the rear.

r. Color team attention: Being at parade rest, the command is "Color Team—Attention." At the command "Attention," resume the position of order arms.

s. Rifle salute: The command is "Rifle—Salute."

(1) Being at right shoulder arms, the command is "Salute." Carry the left hand smartly to the small of the stock, forearm horizontal, palm of the hand down, thumb and fingers extended and joined, first joint of the forefinger touching the rear end of the receiver of the M1 rifle or the end of the cocking piece of the M1903 rifle; look toward the person saluted. On the count of two, cut away the left hand smartly to the side; turn the head and eyes to the front.

(2) Being at order arms or trail arms, at the command "Salute," carry the left hand smartly to the right side, palm of hand down, thumb and fingers extended and joined, forearm and wrist straight, first joint of forefinger touching the barrel between the stacking swivel and the muzzle at a point which best suits the conformation of the man, and look toward the person saluted. On the count of two, cut away the left hand smartly to the side; turn the head and eyes to the front.

MILITARY BANDS   There are many military bands on our military bases, posts, and stations in this country and overseas. They are very vital segments of the military establishment and are necessary to provide music for parades, reviews, retreats, ceremonies, entertainment, and for public relations work with the surrounding communities. There is such a variety of work for the military bands and bandsmen that in one instance one Army band called itself Jay's Variety Troupe. At times some directors may concentrate to such an extent on perfecting the musical capabilities of their units that they tend to forget that first and foremost they are a part of the military family.

One military band leader claimed that his men played everything possible on every possible occasion, on the base and in the nearby communities; yet the installation commander showed very little pride in his band and criticized it constantly. The band's daily schedule when not on an assigned performance was a full one: two hours of concert rehearsal, two hours of ensemble and dance band rehearsal, one hour of individual practice, and one hour of glee club rehearsal. To a musician, this is a very heavy schedule and would tax lip endurance; therefore the leader tried to console himself by thinking, "It is impossible for the band to do more; the C.O. doesn't think highly of the musician's profession."

Looking further into the problem the reasons for the military commander's criticisms became quite evident:

1. Musically speaking, the director had a fine band.
2. Militarily speaking, he had a failure.

If no one ever saw his band, merely heard it, all would have been fine, but its military effectiveness was destroyed by its own appearance. Haircuts, uniforms, shoes, hat bills, and the like were not near minimum military levels of neatness. The bandsmen in this unit exhibited extremely poor posture, lines, and footwork. Such provocations from his band, his show unit, are enough to irritate most military commanders.

The military commander thinks, and rightly so, that his band should be the most "spit and polished" outfit in his command—the band should be a showpiece. Nine times out of ten his main interest does not lie in straight musical work but in retreats, and field performances. In other words, when the band is working as a part of his military team. He wants it to show precision linework and footwork and to contain his sharpest service personnel. This particular band leader's mistake was that he thought only of music. He gave all other aspects of the organization insufficient attention and guidance. Once a band leader in the military establishment places less than 50 percent of his time on the military refinement of his unit he may run into trouble.

To develop a military band necessitates action. It requires inspections, close order drills, and band drills in daily doses. A military band leader has an eight-hour day, when not on another assigned military task, to perfect his organization. A schedule to accomplish the stated objectives might be as follows:

0800 to 0900	Individual, sectional, and ensemble practice
0915 to 1030	Entire band working outside as elements on linework, footwork, formations, etc. without music
1045 to 1200	Glee club and dance band rehearsal
1300 to 1400	Entire band outside with instruments working on lines, maneuvers, formations, etc.
1415 to 1545	Concert rehearsal
1600 to 1700	Care and cleaning of instruments, uniforms, and quarters

Each and every morning a light quarters and personnel inspection should be conducted and a stand-by inspection should be held once per week, regardless of whether or not directives require that frequency of inspections.

Many military band leaders who read this suggested routine will say, "The musicians won't stand for that." At least 75 percent of the shortcomings of military bands are due to the band leader. He is appointed to accomplish one task: to develop a good military band. The services have provided for a great concert band in each of its branches and they are stationed in Washington, D.C. They are designed to be the finest of concert bands; the other bands are created, in most part, to be military marching musical units.

If the leader desires the backing of the military commander, he should give him the sharpest military outfit under his command. Once the militarization procedure begins it will increasingly gain momentum as the bandsmen realize the benefits of the transformation.

In addition to a more balanced rehearsal schedule for a military band, which will give the "military element" its proper weight, there are other factors that the military band director has at his command to "highlight" his unit. Here, as in any other endeavor, dividends are acquired commensurate with the investment. To determine the amount of his own investment every leader should answer the following questions according to his own band's activities:

1. How often does your band play a formal retreat ceremony? Perhaps it is scheduled by higher authority once per week or twice per month. If so scheduled does your band play any retreats in addition to those required? The area for retreat is usually a very select spot in

front of the military commander's headquarters. This affords an opportunity to put the band before the officers of the installation more often than is required. This will not go unnoticed: these extra retreats will be discussed by the officers and men.

2. Have you taken it upon yourself, in the proper season, to initiate an open-air twilight concert where the personnel can bring their families and sit on the lawn? This, too, will bring the unit much favorable comment. Concerning any open-air concert series several things must be kept in mind:

a. One must not expect a landslide turnout at the beginning. The audience will increase as the caliber of the program warrants.

b. The concert should be held on a set evening of the week and not changed each week. Care should be taken not to select an evening the clubs have their regularly scheduled events.

c. Many band leaders feel that a good symphonic program is adequate—this is not so. A much broader program is necessary to hold and then recapture the audience from concert to concert. The evening should be an interesting one for a mixed audience. A few suggestions along these lines would be as follows:

(1) Don't hold a stiff formal affair. Have a good master of ceremonies. He should be a person who is able to involve the audience in the game for the evening. Let the M.C. compliment the women on their suntans, being better cooks than the military cooks, etc. Let him ask how many states are represented by the different hometowns, etc. Ways to interest the audience in the game are endless.

(2) Check with the personnel services officer for special acts to put in the show. A baton twirler, a magician, an animal act; anything to add variety and interest.

(3) Select the music for the concert very carefully and always remember that most people are not musicians and would much rather hear light numbers than heavy ones, especially when outdoors.

(4) Be certain to work up several good comedy numbers and perhaps even a young children's number where they can join hands and circle. This may sound foolish, but whether it does or not, it has audience appeal.

3. What does your unit do during the football season? Does it go to its designated seating area on game days and from there play its music as the occasion arises? What does it do during the half-time period? Does it play from the stands or does it get out on the field and march up and down and perhaps form a spiral or some other ineffective formation? The football game permits the band to demonstrate its musical and military precision. Prepare a good 7½-to-10-minute show for the games and let the responsible people know that the band has a show and wants to go on. In this text there is much material on formation and maneuver design techniques. It can be utilized by military bands just as effectively as by civilian marching musical units.

4. During the formal reviews held, does your band sound off in place or does it troop the line? In either case it is missing another opportunity to gain recognition. The sound off and trooping the line is

a time to show off the band. Instead of just trooping the line, why not a maneuver like operation scatter or the company front described in this text? Don't ever believe that it can't be done because of regulations. In 90 percent of the cases permission is easily obtained. There are two very important factors to be considered for such maneuvers:

a. Be certain that the formation or maneuver does not disturb the troops, i.e. do not miscalculate the necessary performance area.

b. The time element for trooping the line is short. Plan this variation to be executed in about the same time as a regular troop the line. In other words, make it a good military tactic—hit them fast and move out. One military unit did this very thing at the retirement review for a four-star general and the results were marvelous.

Actually there are many other things that could be discussed here concerning a military band but they would be of narrower scope, peculiar to some base or post. The target to shoot at is twofold:

1. Musical excellence.
2. Military precision and sharpness.

A value less than 50 percent of the whole placed on the military aspect will run you into trouble with many officers of the installation. Don't ever give them reason to ask, "Is this a military band?"

6

Parades and contests

TIPS FOR COMMITTEES PLANNING PARADES

The pitfalls and perils possible in every parade are numerous. Ninety percent of the problems can be prevented by a parade planning committee that is fully cognizant of the requirements of marching musical units as well as other parade column elements. The first fact to be realized by the committee is that the composition of a good parade is extremely complex. The items to be considered number in the thousands. Several adverse conditions that create problems for marching units are presented here together with suggested preventive measures:

1. Parade starting time

a. Problem: A parade starts long after the scheduled time due to mass confusion during the initial grouping of the elements.

b. Solution: Correct planning by the committee and providing for enough command posts, manned by informed coordinators, will prevent this. Even in a minutely planned event, the coordinators will have to answer an endless variety of questions and perhaps handle some emergencies.

2. Scheduling the positioning time for individual units

a. Problem: It often happens that all marching units are requested to assemble at one specified time. For short parade columns this is no problem, but in very long parade columns marching units that are not in the first portion of the parade will have waiting periods. For the units near the end of the colmun it may mean a delay of hours. In a parade with one hundred elements, where all marching units are ordered to be in place at the same time, the ninetieth element would move to the I.P. (initial point) approximately one and one half hours after the lead unit departs the I.P.

b. Solution: The planning committee should stagger the positioning times of the participating marching units. A good rule of thumb to follow is that it takes approximately one minute to insert each element in the parade column at the I.P.

3. Hills, turns, and narrow streets

a. Problem: A parade route is selected that extends over very narrow, hilly, and/or twisting streets—usually to favor some preferred group.

b. Solution: The committee should make a special point of plotting the route. Several of the members should then walk (not ride) the route to judge the wisdom of their selection. This must be completed far enough in advance to allow for alterations without upsetting published plans. See the section titled "Planning a Parade Column."

4. Rough pavement

a. Problem: A parade route is laid out over uneven street surfaces such as cobblestones.

b. Solution: Select a route to avoid very rough streets. A musician playing an instrument and observing his alignment can step into a one-inch hole with enough impact to temporarily ruin his lip.

5. Horses

a. Problem: The marching units following a troop of horses run a demoralizing obstacle course.

b. Solution: Horses should be located somewhere behind the last marching unit. Horses add a fine touch to a mixed-element parade but they are not as important as marching musical units.

6. Fire engines

a. Problem: A fire engine blaring its siren or klaxon and drowning out a band's best musical efforts.

b. Solution: Fire engines should be positioned a minimum of 150 feet from the nearest marching musical unit. The committee should outlaw the use of sirens and klaxons. (The fire engines can flash their lights.)

7. Spacing between two marching musical units

a. Problem: Drum corps and/or bands within interference distance of each other experience music and cadence clashes.

b. Solution: In parades the minimum distance between two marching musical units should be 300 feet. This is the least distance at which a clash can be prevented. It also gives each unit an opportunity to hold center stage as it passes the audience.

8. Parade column movement delays

a. Problem: Units that execute unscheduled maneuvers cause a sporadic rate of movement for all following elements.

b. Solution: The planning committee should distribute a list of rules for the event which outlaws unscheduled maneuvers that interfere with the steady forward movement of the parade column.

9. The setting sun

a. Problem: An afternoon parade route is laid out from east to west, where the setting sun blinds the marchers and results in mediocre performances.

b. Solution: The planning committee should select afternoon parade routes that will avoid blinding the marchers. Do not lay out the line of march to the west for a late afternoon parade.

10. Floodlights at the reviewing stand

a. Problem: A night parade in which the reviewing stand is boxed in by giant flood and spotlights at ground level effectively blinding the approaching parade elements.

b. Solution: The committee should position the reviewing stand under good street lighting or have floodlights mounted high overhead.

11. The last unit in the parade column

a. Problem: A band marching as the last element of a parade column often takes affectionate or prankish abuse from the crowd closing in from behind.

b. Solution: The committee should always provide for several motorized vehicles, preferably police cars, as the last element of a parade column.

12. The placement of transportation

a. Problem: A parade route terminates far from its starting point, and the various units of transportation are parked back in the starting area.

b. Solution: The committee should route the parade to terminate near its starting point or arrange to relocate the transportation near the end of the parade route. If relocated, all units should be informed of the post-parade position of their vehicles before the day of the parade.

13. The rate of march

a. Problem: A parade column moves too slowly or too rapidly.

b. Solution: The committee should place a special group of seasoned marchers at the head of the parade to set a steady pace. The pace should be a minimum of 120 and a maximum of 130 steps per minute.

When the participating elements are lined up for a parade, it is too late to change the parade column sequence, march orders, or the general routing—it is just too risky. Action must be taken far enough in advance to make the desired changes with the least confusing effect. Never has the old suggestion "An ounce of prevention is worth a pound of cure" been more applicable than to the case in point. The primary responsibility for the planning is that of the parade committee.

Tips on parades for directors of marching musical units

The most exact and detailed plans of a parade committee cannot encompass every factor that may confront a band or drum corps in a parade. Several actions should be taken previous to the parade by the unit leader. There may also be confrontations in the actual parade when the director should take some action in the best interest of his unit. Several such items warrant consideration:

1. Proper weather/uniform combinations

a. Problem: Marchers suffering from abnormal cold or heat during the parade.

b. Solution: A thoughtful director, acting through his staff, will always obtain a good weather report of the activity area and advise the proper dress combination for the event. (See Chapter 7 on uniforms.)

2. Time and location itinerary

a. Problem: Bandsmen searching for their unit or some other important point in the parade area or being unaware of event times.

b. Solution: Once the director receives the parade committee's instruction sheet he should make out a detailed itinerary for his unit with all conditions, times, and locations specified.

3. Foot blisters

a. Problem: Musicians finishing a parade with foot blisters and other foot problems.

b. Solution: In order to prevent this the band members should be schooled on the importance of the correctly sized shoes, the proper socks, and foot powder.

4. Varying rates or stoppages in the movement of the parade column.

a. Problem: The rate of march causing a jam-up of units making it impossible to continue a reasonable rate of advance.

b. Solution: When the interval to the preceding unit is closed up the director should halt his unit and wait until a 300-foot interval develops in front. He can then resume the march and correct the problem at least for several thousand feet. A director should not half-step his unit in order to keep moving. No director is ever expected to put his organization in a bad light or some impossible situation. If any such condition arises the leader should take immediate action to correct it as gracefully as possible.

There are other factors, many others, which each director must face and resolve or his unit will operate at less than its normal capability and efficiency during parades. A wise director will have his staff study conditions continually to improve the environment in which his unit operates.

PLANNING A PARADE COLUMN

It often happens that a member of a chamber of commerce, police department, fraternal order, or musical organization is asked to act as chairman and supervise the planning of a parade for some community festivity. The occasion may be a firemen's bazaar. Veterans' Day, one of the football bowl games, or one of a hundred other events that call for a parade to highlight the festivities. Most communities which hold celebrations of any kind usually consider the parade the feature event.

The requirements for all parades are similar; therefore, a general plan which can be modified to fit local conditions will cover all such occasions. There are definite tasks that must be done, and they must be accomplished in a certain order. Since the chairman actually plans and directs the total effort through a staff he must recruit a number of assistants, but before he is able to determine the extent of the assistance required he must be given a good idea of the type and size of the parade desired by the city fathers or festivities committee. An outline of the chairman's duties is as follows:

1. Recruiting the staff
   a. The first steps are extremely important.
      (1) Determine the number of parade committees required.
      (2) Determine the number of aides needed.
      (3) Select dependable men and women who will actually carry out the tasks assigned. The selection of a competent staff is probably the most decisive move the chairman will make; 99 percent of the detail work will be handled by the people in the different committees.

2. Assignment of staff duties

    a. Following the selection of the personnel for the committees, a meeting should be called, leaders appointed for each committee, and responsibilities assigned as follows:

        (1) Committee of division coordinators and assistants

            (a) To assist in planning the parade route and parade column.

            (b) To operate division command posts before and during the parade.

        (2) Liaison committee

            (a) To work with the police.

            (b) To control the floats.

            (c) To monitor the fire engines.

            (d) To assist the nonmusical marching units.

            (e) To work with musical marching units.

            (f) To assist with the reviewing stand arrangements.

        (3) Correspondence committee

            (a) To invite elements to participate.

            (b) To send information to participants.

            (c) To answer any inquiries.

        (4) Arrangements committee

            (a) To arrange for necessary lunches.

            (b) To arrange for dressing rooms.

            (c) To arrange for lavatory facilities.

            (d) To arrange for storage accommodations.

        (5) Publicity committee

            (a) To advertise the event by posters and newspapers.

            (b) To publicize the event by radio and television.

        (6) Treasury committee

            (a) To arrange for funds.

            (b) To allocate funds.

    b. Once the parade chairman has appointed the various committee members and leaders, he should instruct them that prior to the next meeting (approximately one week) each leader must outline a plan to cover his committee's part of the total operation.

3. The work of the staff

    a. A second general meeting is necessary to assure that each committee leader really understands his job. This is demonstrated when each committee leader presents a broad workable plan for carrying out the task assigned to him. The chairman and the committee members should offer improvements, modifications, and limitations. Committee leaders should be permitted to formulate their own plans initially. They may come up with some great ideas. Several meetings may be necessary to resolve everything for this phase of the work.

    b. Subsequent to this series of meetings the committee leaders and aides must do the legwork in order to firm up the various requirements. A few examples of such duties are:

        (1) The parade route must be planned. This is the task of the chairman, division coordinators, and the police liaison committee.

(2) The various elements scheduled to be in the parade column must be listed. This compilation is the task of the correspondence committee.

(3) Parking, toilet, storage, luncheon facilities, etc., must be provided by the arrangements committee.

(4) Maps must be drawn by the division coordinators and reproduced by the correspondence committee.

4. Formulating the parade column

a. By this time some two to four months may have elapsed since the chairman was appointed. Enough statistics, charts, etc., should be on hand to formulate the parade column. The chairman and the division coordinators must determine the position of each element in the parade column, the intervals between elements, and so forth.

b. A hypothetical list of elements that have entered the parade comes from the correspondence committee as follows:

(1) 15 floats

(2) 10 fire engines

(3) 1 mock locomotive

(4) 2 veterans groups

(5) 2 ladies auxiliary troops

(6) 1 unit of police on foot

(7) 4 units of servicemen—Army, Navy, Marine, and Air Force—with service bands and equipment

(8) 50 children on decorated bicycles

(9) The parade marshal's entourage

(10) 11 musical marching units, other than service bands

(11) American Legion marchers

(12) Local police, riding

(13) Drum majorettes' school

c. The order in which the elements are placed in the parade column plays a heavy role in determining the success of the parade.

(1) Reread the section titled "Tips for Committees Planning Parades" and guard against the adverse situations mentioned.

(2) The front element should be a group on foot in order to set the pace for the entire column. This group can be police or flag bearers or any unit that will set a steady pace (120 minimum to 130 maximum). It too often happens that squad cars, the Queen's Float, or motorcycles head the parade; but an automobile or motorcycle cannot set a definite marching pace. If a motorized unit must head the parade it must maintain a speed of approximately 3.5 miles per hour.

d. From the hypothetical list of entries, a parade column might be formed as follows:

1st Division
14 units

Pacesetting unit on foot
Police band
Official entourage and police
Queen's float
Army band
Army troops and equipment
Marine band
Marine troops and equipment
Navy band
Navy troops and equipment
Air Force band
Air Force troops and equipment
First veterans group
Second veterans group

2nd Division
14 units

Band
1 troop of boy scouts
Float
Drum and bugle corps
Float
Float
Float
Band
1 troop of boy Scouts
Float
Band
Float
Float
Float

3rd Division
13 units

Drum and bugle corps
Ladies auxiliary troops
Float
Band
Float
Float
Float
Drum and bugle corps
Ladies auxiliary troops
Float
Band
Float
Children on bikes

4th Division
12 units

Band
Drum majorettes' school
5 fire engines
5 fire engines

5th Division
4 units
{
American Legion drum and bugle corps
American Legion marchers
1 mock locomotive
Police car or 2 police motorcycles

e. Spacing of the units in the parade column
   (1) Minimum intervals necessary
      (a) Between divisions: 250 feet
      (b) Between elements: a minimum of 75 feet except bands, which should have a 150-foot interval ahead of them. See *Diagram 55.*

Diagram 55 / **Parade column spacing**

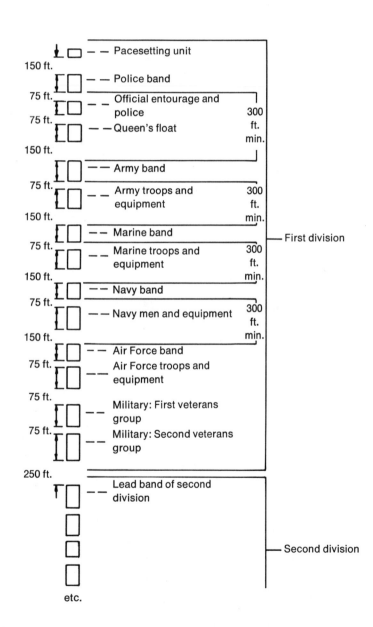

(2) Division structure and spacing

1st Division

(a) Pacesetting unit
150 feet
(b) Police band
75 feet
(c) Official Entourage & Police
75 feet
(d) Queen's float
150 feet
(e) Army band
75 feet
(f) Army troops followed by equipment
150 feet
(g) Marine band
75 feet
(h) Maine troops followed by equipment
150 feet
(i) Navy band
75 feet
(j) Navy troops followed by equipment
150 feet
(k) Air Force band
75 feet
(l) Air Force troops followed by equipment
75 feet
(m) 1st veterans group
75 feet
(n) 2nd veterans group

250 feet

2nd Division

(a) Band
75 feet
(b) Boy scouts
75 feet
(c) Float
150 feet
(d) Drum and bugle corps
75 feet
(e) Float
75 feet
(f) Float
75 feet
(g) Float
150 feet
(h) Band
75 feet

(i) Troop of Boy Scouts
75 feet
(j) Float
150 feet
(k) Band
75 feet
(l) Float
75 feet
(m) Float
75 feet
(n) Float

250 feet

3rd Division

(a) Drum and bugle corps
75 feet
(b) One troop of ladies auxiliary
75 feet
(c) Float
150 feet
(d) Band
75 feet
(e) Float
75 feet
(f) Float
75 feet
(g) Float
150 feet
(h) Drum and bugle corps
75 feet
(i) One troop of ladies auxiliary
75 feet
(j) Float
150 feet
(k) Band
75 feet
(l) Float
75 feet
(m) Children on bikes

250 feet

4th Division
- (a) Band
  - 75 feet
- (b) Drum majorettes' school
  - 75 feet
- (c) Fire engine
  - 75 feet
- (d) Fire engine
  - 75 feet
- (e) Fire engine
  - 75 feet
- (f) Fire engine
  - 75 feet
- (g) Fire engine
  - 75 feet
- (h) Fire engine
  - 75 feet
- (i) Fire engine
  - 75 feet
- (j) Fire engine
  - 75 feet
- (k) Fire engine
  - 75 feet
- (l) Fire engine

250 feet

5th Division
- (a) American Legion drum and bugle corps
  - 75 feet
- (b) American Legion marchers
  - 75 feet
- (c) Mock locomotive
  - 75 feet
- (d) Police car or 2 police motorcycles

f. As soon as the parade column has been formulated a recheck should be made to ascertain the following:

(1) That a pacing unit is leading the parade.

(2) That every marching group has a band leading it.

(3) That the spacings show distinct breaks between units, sections of a division, and divisions.

(4) That the musical organizations are separated to prevent conflict with each other.

(5) That the music is spread throughout the entire column by proper spacing of the bands and drum corps.

(6) That the armed services are in the column according to correct service protocol.

(7) That the queen's float is placed near the head of the column in order that it may be pulled out at the reviewing stand.

5. Duties of the parade committees

The parade committees are extremely important and each has a great deal of work to do. The tasks these committees should accomplish are as follows:

a. Parade chairman: He is the foreman of the project. His major tasks, after the committees are operating, are to see that each committee is motivated; does its job and does it correctly; and that the entire project is always coordinated. In many cases there are co-chairmen in charge of a parade; this is a tactical error. There can be only one chairman or commander of any type of organization if it is to run efficiently.

b. Division coordinators and assistants: one coordinator and two assistants per division, whose tasks are:

(1) To check in detail the parade route possibilities and to help map the parade route.

(2) To help plan the parade column.

(3) To set up their division command post at the head of their division assembly area on the day of the parade. Command posts should be marked on a large sign placed in a conspicuous location at the head of each division. Either the division coordinator or an assistant should be at the command post continually for a minimum of two hours before the assembly time on the day of the parade. This is necessary in order to answer all questions and guide all units in that division into place. The facility can be austere, a table under a tree or a pick-up truck, but because of the heavy requirements for good communication there should be a phone or walkie-talkie available.

c. Liaison with police: three men who must:

(1) Arrange bus and truck parking spaces for elements of divisions in the designated division areas.

(2) Arrange for police escorts to guide incoming elements into the proper area. This is extremely important in a large city.

(3) Arrange for one ambulance and several first aid stations.

(4) Arrange for radio cars and motorcycles to be spaced in the assembly and parade areas for communications.

(5) Arrange to have the entire parade route, assembly area, dismissal area, and parking area well posted with signs, stating "No Parking" between such and such hours on a certain day. (These posters should be in place forty-eight hours before the assembly time.)

(6) Arrange to have all parade areas blocked to traffic.

d. Liaison with floats: three men who must:

(1) Have one rubber-tired tractor with rope stand by to tow off break-downs.

(2) Caution float personnel about fire hazards. Advise that fire extinguishers must be carried on each float.

(3) Advise all vehicle drivers to check their gas, battery, cooling system, etc.

e. Liaison with fire engines: three men who must:

(1) Arrange for placement of engines.

(2) Caution against use of sirens. (Lights are permissible.)

(3) Arrange for dispersal of engines at the end of the parade.

f. Liaison with nonmusical marching units: two men who should:

(1) Advise unit leaders of the pace length and cadence of the lead element of the parade.

(2) Have foot powder, Band-aids and shoelaces available for use.

(3) Remain with the units until departure from the I.P. to cope with unforeseen problems.

g. Liaison with musical marching units: four men who should:

(1) Make up an emergency kit containing the following items:

(a) 4 pairs of snare drum sticks

(b) 4 snare drum slings

(c) 2 bass drum beaters

(d) 1 drum major's baton

(e) 5 tubes of lip ice

(f) 1 roll adhesive tape

(g) 1 roll friction tape

(h) 1 roll scotch tape

(i) 2 packages of safety pins

(j) 2 sewing kits

(k) 2 boxes of Band-aids

(2) Brief drum majors on the following points.

(a) The I.P. (initial point) where the bands begin to play.

(b) The location of the reviewing stand.

(c) The forward rate of movement of the drum.

(3) Remain with the bands until departure from the I.P. to cope with unforeseen problems.

h. Liaison with reviewing stand: three men who should:

(1) Make certain that the reviewing stand is on the right side of the column movement, if at all possible.

(2) Make certain that the reviewing stand is approximately no farther than two miles from the I.P. and no closer than one mile.

(3) Have a large sign visible to the parade column: "Reviewing Stand—300 Feet."

(4) Make certain that the position of the reviewing stand affords a minimum of 300 feet of straight approach and a minimum of 200 feet of straight departure. It is very important to have the reviewing stand on the right-hand side and equally important to have the correct approach and departure.

(5) Arrange for a powerful public address system to announce the units as they appear. A mistake here can be very embarrassing to everyone. Such embarrassment can be prevented by having a radio car at the I.P. obtain the name of each element as it leaves the I.P. and transmit it to the reviewing stand. The announcer's assistant can verify the names against prepared lists. Walkie-talkies are also fine for this purpose.

(6) Arrange for an announcer to handle the PA system. Make certain he is thoroughly briefed.

(7) Be careful to seat people of rank according to protocol. Mistakes have caused much embarrassment in the past.

(8) Be certain to ascertain the rank of the person receiving the review. This is very important to the military bands for ruffles and flourishes, if applicable. Make certain each division coordinator has this information.

(9) Arrange for any ceremonies following the parade with the division coordinators and elements involved.

i. Liaison for arrangements: two men per division who should:

(1) Arrange facilities as applicable for their division to change clothing, wash, store instrument cases, etc. Be sure to have facilities to hang up clothes. Put guards on these areas or arrange to have them locked while the parade is in progress.

(2) Arrange for sufficient and well-marked toilet facilities.

(3) Ascertain which units must be fed and work out a complete schedule.

(4) Arrange for first aid stations.

j. Publicity committee: four men who should:

(1) Gather all possible pictures of and information on the participating elements.

(2) Work with newspapers, radio, and television to assure good coverage. Make certain that a diagram of the parade is given to the local newspapers one week previous to the event.

(3) Arrange for posters and display cards for billboards and store windows.

(4) Arrange for pictures and human interest items on the day of the parade.

6. Parade route and stationing diagram

a. Study the sample parade route depicted in this book *(Diagram 56)* and note the factors imperative to insure a good parade.

(1) Few turns in the parade route.

(2) Location of the reviewing stand. (Give each unit the time necessary to settle down, and yet still be fresh when passing.)

(3) Location of transportation. (End the parade circuit near the unit's transportation.)

(4) Dispersal points for local units. (Let the hometown units out of the parade at advantageous points.)

(5) Division forming areas. (Provide parking facilities.)

b. Furnish each member of the various committees and the police with copies of the parade route and stationing diagram as soon as possible. See *Diagram 56.*

7. Miscellaneous notes

a. The parade route may be planned before the units of the parade column are known. The parade route simply should take advantage of the most appropriate streets and facilities.

b. After a unit has informed the correspondence committee that it will enter the parade, it should receive specific instructions by mail from the committee. For example, instructions to the Bailey High School Band:

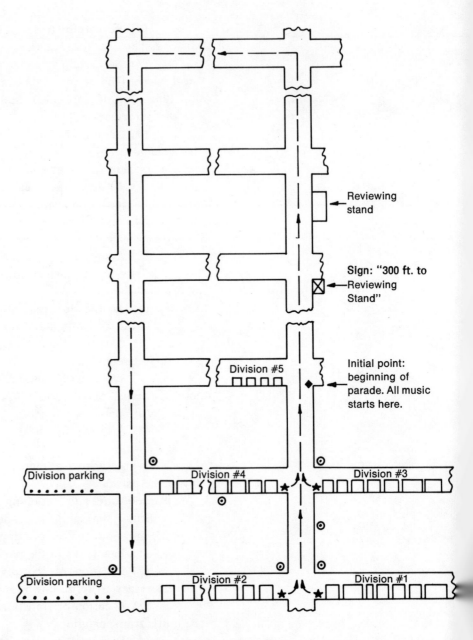

Reviewing stand

Sign: "300 ft. to Reviewing Stand"

Initial point: beginning of parade. All music starts here.

Division #5

Division #4

Division #3

Division parking

Division #2

Division #1

Division parking

Diagram 56 / **Model parade route and stationing diagram**

KEY:

⊙ Toilets

★ Division command posts

(1) You are in Division Number 3.

(2) Your division command post is on the corner of Apple Avenue and 3rd Street.

(3) Your division coordinator is Mr. K. Doe.

(4) Your parking area is on Apple Street back of the division forming area. (It will be marked.)

(5) Your dressing and storage area is the gymnasium of the Milbourne Junior High at 8th and Hogate Street. (Advise you to dress before lunch.)

(6) Your unit will be fed at the Victory Restaurant at 4th and Hogate Street at 12 noon.

(7) Your unit should be in position at 2:00 PM for **final** check.

(8) The pacesetting unit for the parade will march with thirty-inch paces at a cadence of 128.

(9) The parade starts at 2:30 EST on 12 April, 19—.

c. In order that the Queen may see the parade, her float should be pulled out of the parade at the reviewing stand. (Do not let her float block the parade route.) Her float can then rejoin the parade immediately behind the mock locomotive.

d. Each musical unit should have a 150-foot minimum interval in front of it, so it can be seen and heard. (Never forget that the bands are the workhorses of the parade.)

e. A hundred incidentals will arise that can be handled by the chairman and committees by the use of common sense and a little effort.

f. These ideas or techniques and procedures on planning a parade column are enumerated to assist the parade committees, but it is highly improbable that the exact format suggested here can be used anywhere. Minor modifications and adjustments to fit local conditions are always required for any general scheme.

A MUSICAL PARADE ROUTINE

It is important for a marching musical organization to maintain alignment, posture, discipline, and positive action in a parade. The judgment of every member of the audience is formulated by what is seen and heard in less than ninety seconds, which is the approximate time a marching unit is exposed to any part of the audience. Anything that will detract from these ninety seconds must be eliminated. It is well for every director to reflect again on the odd but true, often stated fact that "Ninety percent of a parade audience hears with its eyes." Plan every parade with this in mind. The music to be performed during a parade must accentuate the marching routine—not detract from it.

In planning a musical parade routine there are as many "musts" as "don'ts." The "don'ts" must be enumerated because their usage has become common practice over a period of years. The "musts" will be spelled out because they are the means to attain the ninety-second perfection that every marching musical unit should seek.

Examples of current procedures

1. All too frequently we find a parade unit in which the members carry march folios containing ten to twenty marches. These are played one after another with any number of drum cadences in between. The length of the cadences and the start and cut-off of the marches are left to the discretion of the drum major. The men literally stumble along, attempting to read the music, keep in step, and watch for signals from the drum major. A few may even forget to turn the music or drop it in an effort to turn it. Regardless of the effort, the result is always the same—a bad start and a poor march rendition, to say nothing of the alignment, posture, or discipline.

2. Perhaps a unit has five marches in its folio, numbered one to five. When the drum major decides on one of the marches, he holds

up his hand with one, two, three, four, or five fingers extended. The men in the front rank make the correct selection—many in the rear guess at it. Or they may inquire from the men beside or ahead of them what selection will be played next. The only result from this system is confusion and at best uncertainty.

Don't set up deterrents that will assure a poor marching performance. Look for and eliminate each point of confusion, each weak part of the operation. Here are six deterrents that confuse the members and weaken the performance of a band on parade:

1. Playing too many different marches.
2. Using an indefinite number of drum cadences between marches.
3. Following no firm order in changing from one march to another.
4. Reading music, which takes attention from cover and alignment.
5. Reading the music, which results in poor marching posture.
6. Neglecting to pay attention to the signals of the drum major, which results in poor footwork and maneuver response.

Actually, playing members of any marching unit should have only two items to be concerned about in a parade.

1. Alignment
2. Drum major signals

Nothing must detract from these two items. All other actions should be mechanical or performed automatically. Reading music while marching certainly will detract since the process is not mechanical.

Now on the positive side. It is really quite simple to create a fine marching musical organization which will at all times present its best during the ninety seconds it is exposed to its audience. The key to success in any parade is to use a set procedure which will eliminate as many confusing elements as possible.

The system to keep the confusing factors to a minimum is a *musical parade routine*. Favorable factors of such a system are:

1. There are no music folios required.
2. There is a set number of cadences established between marches.
3. The musical routine is set and requires no guesswork as to what is to be played next.
4. The alignment and the drum major can be observed 100 percent of the time.
5. The drum major is not concerned with music signals except for the initial start and unscheduled cuts; therefore, he can pay full attention to guiding the unit along the parade route.

One might say that there is a disadvantage because the music has to be memorized. Every marching musical band should always have at least two memorized marchers ready to use at all times.

A musical parade routine encompassing minimum confusion, thereby permitting the unit to perform at top efficiency, is suggested as follows:

Musical parade routine

Fanfare (played only at the I.P.)
1. "American Patrol"
   Four cadences—Roll-off
2. "National Emblem"
3. "Downfall of Paris"—Roll-off

This is an example of the longest musical parade routine that should be used. In order to understand fully the detailed workings of the example above, it is necessary to analyze it section by section.

Fanfare: At the very beginning of the parade, or at the I.P., the parade column is a little unstable because the different units are jockeying to get their proper spaces and get in the swing of things. From its assembly area point your unit follows the preceding unit very closely to the I.P. on a drum tap, disregarding the interval that must be maintained during the parade. It is stopped at the I.P. and aligned; this should take no more than a few seconds. The drum major then faces the unit, and at such time when he will pick up the proper interval between his unit and the preceding one in the parade, he verbally commands, "Fanfare." Still facing the unit he uses the baton signal to start the fanfare. The band does not move during the fanfare, but stands at attention. The fanfare should not be longer than twelve seconds but it should be big and powerful. Not only is this fanfare very impressive to the audience, which sees a well-aligned unit and hears a stirring introduction, but it has a great psychological effect on the members. It gives the bandsmen a very definite beginning for the event. An exact and well-executed start on any project is a very important factor for good performance.

First March—"American Patrol": At the completion of the fanfare, the musicians pick up the march immediately. (No signal from the drum major is necessary.) The entire unit steps off on the first beat of the march. In this march music, as in all others used on parade, second endings should be used. A musician will have more endurance by playing a brief period and then taking a short rest. In addition, playing all second endings allows more activity or animation in any one parade than playing the entire march as written.

Four Cadences—Roll-off: Following the march music, without a signal from the drum major, the percussion section plays a series of four cadences. (This is one of the indisputable reasons for building a powerful, well-trained percussion section.) At the end of the series of cadences, with no signal from the drum major, the percussion section executes a roll-off. (The simple roll-off is overworked and as far as the sound goes leaves much to be desired. Any good drummer can write an original roll-off. Every band should have a special one.)

Second March—"National Emblem": Immediately following the roll-off, with no signal from the drum major, the entire band begins the second march of the musical parade routine. In this march all second endings are also used.

"Downfall of Paris": Following the march music, with no signal from

the drum major, the entire percussion section plays the "Downfall of Paris," using the second endings. The "Downfall," as it is commonly called, is one of the best percussion numbers ever written for use in a parade. If executed correctly, it has a driving power that is enormous. Of course there are other good percussion numbers which can be used, such as "The Wrecker's Daughter," "Connecticut Half Time," etc. After the completion of the "Downfall," with no signal from the drum major, the percussion section executes a roll-off and the unit picks up the music of the first march or, in other words, starts to repeat the musical parade routine. The above comprises the entire musical parade routine. It should carry the unit forward about one half mile, if moving steadily. The fanfare is not used to begin the routing for the second time or at any time other than the departure from the I.P.

General notes on this routine

1. Every marching musical organization should have a musical parade routine ready to put in operation at all times. This means practice and more practice. The music for the entire routine must be memorized and then practiced outdoors.

2. The musical parade routine should be posted on the unit bulletin board at all times. After the memorized marches or cadences have been used for some time they can be replaced, one at a time, by new music. The beauty of this idea is that the organization becomes familiar with the sequence. This sequence should never change.

3. In cases of stoppages in the movement of the parade column, after the event is under way, the only sensible thing for the drum major to do is to bring the unit to mark time, halt it, cut the music, and give the men parade rest. In order to get started again the drum major instructs the men verbally to pick up the musical parade routine at a given point such as the "Downfall" or the "National Emblem." After that, the sequence is continued and the organization can proceed without confusion.

4. Not only does a musical parade routine allow the members to concentrate on alignment and the drum major but another impressive advantage can be gained. With an exact music sequence the playing members find it easier to bring up their instruments together at the beginning of a number.

5. If one desires to have a great marching band, one feature must be added to the musical parade routine. The most powerful and best number should be played to pass the reviewing stand. With a little practice this number can be inserted in the sequence so as to prevent the unit passing the reviewing stand merely using cadences or the tail end of a march. As the unit proceeds along the parade route using the musical parade routine the drum major must carefully observe the approach to the reviewing stand. At a proper distance (say 250 feet) from the stand he should signal that the feature number is coming by holding his baton high in the air and waving it back and forth. (See "alert signal" in the section titled "Drum Major.") He does this for about fifty feet to make sure that he has the attention

of the entire unit; he then cuts the music, as described in the section titled "Drum Major." The music is cut on the baton signal regardless of what is being played and immediately, with no additional signal, the drums roll off and the "feature music" is begun. The unit passes the reviewing stand at its best. This number can be a part of the regular routine, and if it is, the routine can then be continued in sequence after the completion of the feature number. If, on the other hand, the feature number is not in the musical parade routine, the "Downfall" can follow it with no signal from the drum major. The sequence of the routine can thus be started again without faltering. This embellishment must, of course, be practiced, but it is certainly worthwhile.

This is the formula for the musical parade routine; a system to relieve confusion and present the unit as an organization that operates at high efficiency.

COMPETITIONS OF MARCHING MUSICAL UNITS

There are any number of reasons to hold contests at which marching musical units have an opportunity to compete. There are two general types of contests and they are vastly different with regard to performance environment, preparation time, and execution time. The two types are:

1. A parade competition. The event is a parade during which the musical units will be scored as they pass the judges' stand.

2. A field competition. The event is a contest with other similar organizations on a designated area such as a football field. The performance time allotted to each unit ranges anywhere from eight to fifteen minutes. In this situation, which is the ideal one for competition, the contestants are judged upon all phases of their performance, from originality to spirit.

The competition committees

This book has previously emphasized the tremendous volume of work, the detail, the communications, etc., involved in planning a parade. In many respects the planning, organizing, and controlling of a marching musical competition are quite similar. The management structure requiring one chairman, a separate committee for each functional area, and a leader for each committee remains the same. Many of the technical facets, such as dining facilities and dressing rooms, also require the same planning; but others, such as the limited number of entries, stadium liaison, etc., are peculiar to field competitions. The chairman's success in staging an exciting and memorable competition will depend, to a great extent, on his initial action, the selection of his committee members and leaders. The committees required are as follows:

1. Planning committee: two to five members
2. Correspondence committee: two to four members
3. Arrangements committee: ten to thirty members
4. Liaison committee: six to twelve members
5. Command post committee: two for each command post

6. Treasury committee: two members

7. Publicity committee: two members

Duties of the Various Committees

1. Planning committee: it carries out the master planning and overall coordination.

a. The date for the contest should be selected approximately six months in advance. Care must be exercised to ascertain the availability of the stadium and that no similar community event will be held on the same date. However, it may be beneficial to include the competition as a part of some large celebration such as the county fair or the 100th anniversary of the city, etc. An alternate date is necessary in case of inclement weather.

b. The competition time is quite important. From 2 to 5 in the afternoon or 7:30 to 10:30 in the evening is fine. The total competition, including all extra appendages, should never exceed three hours.

c. The number of entries must be carefully controlled. A maximum of ten competitors allow each unit to have twelve minutes on the field. This leaves one hour for the flag ceremonies, awards, and other features.

d. Homogeneity of competitors must be considered. Senior high bands, junior high bands, drum corps, etc., should not be mixed. Judging is impossible under such conditions.

e. Some competition planners select a theme for the competition. If a theme is chosen, it should be a very broad one—for example, the American High School Band, Musical America, Industrial America, and the like. A theme such as the 100th Anniversary of South Branch is much too restrictive.

f. The complete format for the competition must be formulated from the opening ceremonies, through the competition and the closing ceremonies.

2. Correspondence committee: it handles all correspondence to and from those involved in the competition.

a. The initial correspondence requests a unit's participation. It states the time and date, place, size of area, theme, and performance time. It should be mailed six months in advance of the competition date

b. Detailed information should be sent to the participants one month ahead of the event.

    (1) The performance area

        (a) Map and address

        (b) Condition

        (c) Oddities

    (2) The time elements

        (a) Time competition begins

        (b) Minimum performance time

        (c) Maximum performance time

        (d) Time unit takes the field

    (3) Time and location regarding dining facilities

    (4) Storage area for the unit

(5) Seating area for the unit

(6) Lavatory facilities

(7) Location of the command post for the unit

(8) Location of first aid and repair station

(9) Lighting conditions, if at night

    (a) General lighting

    (b) Lighting available upon request; lights out, spots, etc.

(10) Public address system

    (a) Availability to the unit's master of ceremonies

    (b) Fact sheet for professional announcer

(11) List of other participants

(12) Scoring system

(13) General location of judges

3. Arrangements committee: the proper arrangements often make the difference between a good and bad event.

    a. Stadium committee: two persons

    (1) Secures use of the area.

    (2) Obtains all usage rules for stadium.

    (3) Arranges seating.

    (4) Secures dressing and storage areas.

    (5) Marks facilities for recognition.

    (6) Assures condition of turf; grass, markings, insect repellent, etc. (Grass should not be alive with mosquitoes.)

    b. Dining and refreshments: two persons

    (1) See section "Planning a Parade."

    (2) Stadium refreshments are best handled by a regular concession firm or a group such as a ladies auxiliary.

    c. Prizes and trophies

    (1) For a competition of ten bands, there should be three award trophies plus seven small memento plaques.

    (2) All trophies should be engraved with the rank of the award, the competition location, name of event, and date.

    (3) Arrange for gate prizes, if applicable.

    d. Ticket sales (if applicable): five to twenty persons

    (1) Decide upon composition of ticket.

    (2) Arrange for printing.

    (3) Activate network of sales people and sales points.

    (4) Arrange for money and ticket collection.

    e. First Aid and repairs: three persons

    (1) They should be at their stations two hours before, during, and one half hour after the performance time.

    (2) One combination station will suffice in a stadium.

    (3) One first aid specialist and an assistant are a must.

    (4) One well-equipped person to make emergency repairs on uniforms is always an asset.

4. Liaison committee: this committee must ascertain that all those concerned with or involved in the event work together smoothly.

    a. With police: two persons

(1) Plans traffic routes.

(2) Designates parking areas.

(3) Arranges for police in stadium.

b. With civic organizations: two persons

(1) Briefs civic organizations on plans and progress.

(2) Requests specialized assistance as needed.

c. With local schools: two persons

(1) Arranges for a host band to handle any special activities such as the National Anthem.

(2) Arranges dressing rooms, lavatories, and storage areas.

d. With the competition judges: two persons

(1) Selects the appropriate judges—unbiased, nonparticipating directors; retired directors; military men; artists and performers.

(2) Decides upon the scoring sheets and seating of the judges.

(3) Limits number of judges to a maximum of five and a minimum of three.

(4) Arranges for awards presentation.

5. Command posts: these men act as complete information sources, the chairman's lieutenants, etc., during the competition. They must be well versed on all rules, times, and other aspects of the competition.

a. One command post is required for every 100 bandsmen.

b. Command posts should be manned two hours before the event and during the entire event.

c. They should be well located and clearly marked.

d. They should have telephones or walkie-talkies for proper communications.

e. The facilities need not be grand: a table and chairs make a fine command post for one evening.

6. Treasury: the proper accountability of all funds involved is absolutely necessary.

a. Arrange for handling of funds.

b. Allocate funds.

7. Publicity: good publicity coverage is a necessity for a successful competition.

a. The committee should function as described for the publicity committee for a parade.

b. These committee members should be selected for their knowledge of radio, television, newspaper, magazine, billboard, and placard advertising. Advertising correctly and at the proper moment is a complicated task.

c. A magazine-type pamphlet with pictures of the participants, short interest items from the communities, and advertising makes a fine memento of the event.

The committees as much as the participants determine the degree of success the event will achieve. The more complete and detailed the planning and follow-through prior to the competition date, the better the event will turn out. Even with maximum planning, there will be unforeseen problems and a few emergencies at the time of the contest. Don't panic because of a last-minute emergency!

Notes for directors of participating units

1. At times a marching musical unit enters a special parade or field contest to compete for prizes and trophies. If a good showing is made, this single event that can do more to get school and/or community enthusiasm behind the organization than most directors realize. It is a generally recognized fact that the sponsors and the fans all love a winner. It would, therefore, seem that a director's route is well marked. It is not possible to hobble along all year with poor training, then spend two weeks practicing and expect to win a contest. The members must be kept proficient through scheduled training and then have additional polishing for the competition.

2. The unit's library should have a series of ideas and shows containing standard formations and maneuvers that have been tested and have proved to be outstanding. When the competition is announced, the show is assembled, and the rehearsing can begin. Three or four months are not lost while all concerned strain to formulate some plan for the performance.

3. Facts regarding all aspects of the competition should be gathered.

a. Where in the parade route will the judges' stand be located? The statement has often been made by leaders of the contestants, "We didn't even see the judges' stand until we passed it playing a drum cadence."

b. How large is the performance area? This is extremely important, because a performance must be planned to fit into the available area.

c. How much time is allocated for each contestant? What are the time penalties? A majority of competitions have rules that impose penalties should the performance be less than the minimum or more than the maximum allotted time.

d. What time of day or night will the performance be held? If the performance should be at night and covered by television, there may be a very limited lighted area within which to stay in order to keep the entire performance spotlighted.

e. Will the judges be situated at ground level or on a raised platform? Many formations will not show up advantageously if the judges see them at ground level. For example, if an anchor is formed and the judges are seated at ground level, they would not be able to see the entire picture and could not fully appreciate it even though it might be an expertly executed formation.

4. After the director and his staff have gathered all the information and rules germane to the competition, the unit's performance can be considered.

a. The unit enters a parade where it will be rated as it marches past the judges.

The time element is very short. During this time the competitors must leave a very good impression if they intend to be named a winner. The ranks and files must be straight, the posture good, and the music impressive. The band can be moving along the parade route using its musical parade routine. At some point, not more than two hundred feet from the judges' stand, the drum major can cut off the music. The signal for the cut-off can also be the signal for a roll-off by the percussion section. The entire band can begin its best and most powerful march number and parade by the judges at maximum efficiency. One can readily imagine the impact if a unit executes the 360-degree turn as it passes the judges. (See section "Advanced Footwork.") At the completion of the special number, the entire unit can return to the beginning of its musical parade pattern. The competitive offering has several advantages:

(1) The judges will hear the shift to the special number and it will draw their attention.

(2) A majority of judges will think the unit is well trained, because it is doing something special as it passes their stand.

(3) The organization is at its best musically while being judged.

(4) The three preceding remarks pertain to the music. The ranks, files, postures, and the like must be perfected by diligent outdoor training. It requires practice, but the unit that devotes ample time toward mastering such a procedure will be an outstanding one.

b. The unit enters a field competition where it is judged as it performs in a designated contest arena.

This is the true test of the organization's abilities. When the unit enters such a contest, the planners should collect every piece of information available that will affect the performance. The show must be planned from this information. The sponsor's correspondence committee should supply all the pertinent data to each contestant. Should the committee fail to do this, the director should obtain it through his own resources. With all possible information at hand, the performance for the competition can be formulated. While building the show, it is necessary to remember that the judges will score high for showmanship, precision, originality, and appeal. A lot of action should go into the show. The competitor should not spend fifteen minutes in a few formations playing four or five numbers. The only item the judges can score on such a demonstration is musical ability. A spectacular performance might be constructed as follows:

(1) Start from one end of the field with a fanfare formation; reform the block; run through operation scatter, execute a box reverse at the far end of the field; then form a company front facing the judges or main audience block; go into concert formation and play a short concert number.

(2) Reform the block and do a production number, such as a salute to the services or a history of transportation.

(3) As the band leaves the field it might play a good arrangement of "So Long, It's Been Good To Know You."

(4) A powerful and impressive beginning and ending are necessary because these are two high points of the performance.

This is just one of the many schedules possible for a fast-moving, exciting performance that displays all the talent the unit has.

5. Contest performances of any type boil down to common sense

and a lot of effort; this is the unbeatable combination. In any type of a contest, 50 percent of the effectiveness of the showing the band makes is determined by the advance planning and the maximum use of all the information that can be compiled. The remaining 50 percent is sufficient practice. A final word of advice: Do not allot three to five minutes of the unit's ten-minute time period in contest to a soloist, a baton twirler, rope artist, etc. The judges are scoring a marching musical unit competition, not a solo artist.

JUDGING A CONTEST   It is a civic duty of an experienced person to act as a contest judge when invited to do so. A request from the sponsors of a competition for marching musical units should be deemed an honor. However, too often the qualified person shirks the assignment and the task goes to someone who is not qualified. The use of unqualified personnel is unfair to the contestants. The judges should have backgrounds in the music, military, theatrical, and related fields.

In addition to the proper qualifications, the number of official scorers is an important consideration. A minimum of three judges allows for the all-important averaging effect. A contest should never be scored by a single judge. The single judge would be placed under a severe handicap because he or she would have only one view of the displays and would bear the sole responsibility for naming the winners.

The judges should be placed in various locations that afford different views of the performances. They should not be grouped at a table. Their positions could be set as follows: the first high in the bleachers, the second halfway up in the bleachers, the third about ten feet above ground level, the fourth at ground level and the fifth at one end of the field viewing the performances at right angles. Such positions give the judges different views of the performance. The scores will vary much more than if they are seated together, but this is as it should be. The judges are not only different people with different qualifications and personalities, they are scoring from different perspectives.

Scoring sheets   Even highly qualified persons require some guidance when they are to work as a team; therefore, the judges must be given comprehensive but realistic scoring sheets. The rating sheets must focus attention on the contest, compartmentalize the various aspects of the performance, and assign rating weights to each aspect. Several guidelines on the scoring or rating sheets are as follows:

1. The scoring sheet, one per judge per contestant, should be complete, yet simple, so that 90 percent of the judges' time can be utilized in observing and checking the performance. The score sheet should tell a complete story to the contestants. This will be invaluable as a critique of their performance.

2. All judges should be required to use identical scoring sheets and complete them in their entirety. Here the contestants must realize that

there may be large variations in scores on any item because the judges will be recording independent views and will have different qualifications. A judge trained as a musician may score music differently from one whose main interest is showmanship.

3. The score sheets should be so composed that as soon as a unit has ended its performance, its score can be calculated in several minutes.

4. The individual score sheet should be formulated on a basis of 1,000 points as a maximum for any contestant. The 1,000 points should be divided and assigned to different categories. For example, if 300 points are assigned to the music, a unit would have to execute the music perfectly for its class, in the judges' opinion, to receive 300. The usual score will be below the maximum. The 1,000 points should be divided into compartments that adequately cover all aspects of a competition performance such as:

a. Inspection	100 Points
b. Music	300
c. Originality	100
d. Formations and Maneuvers	300
e. Spirit	100
f. Timing	100
TOTAL	1,000 Points

5. If a performance is perfect, the score is 1,000. Points will be lost on music, timing, and any other noticeable shortcomings so that the final score by a judge for any one band will be below 1,000 points. To illustrate this, it is necessary to consider each item separately.

a. The inspection carries a maximum of 100 points. As one unit completes its performance, the next one should be lined up and be prepared for inspection. One judge should run a close-up inspection on the field. The other judges should check on overall appearance from from their positions. The judge on the field, making the close inspection, checks on:

(1) Uniforms

(2) Shoes

(3) Instrument condition

(4) Postures

(5) Neatness

b. The music is allowed only 300 points of the total score weight, because in a competition of marching musical units, the total spectacle is a much larger factor than the music. Music should be scored on dynamics, intonation, tempo, arrangement, appropriateness, etc.

c. Originality is allotted 100 points. This is an important factor in making a good show and also a big factor to the audience.

d. Formations and maneuvers are allotted 300 points. These not only include the actual performance but indicate the volume of planning and preparation.

e. Spirit is allowed 100 points. It is the vital spark that can lift a contestant to perform above normal capability.

f. Timing is given 100 points since it is important in contests. For example, suppose a time of ten minutes is allocated to each band. Should a unit complete its performance in less than nine minutes, it should be penalized, one point for every second on the minus side of nine minutes and, conversely, one point for every second it exceeds ten minutes.

g. The score sheet for one band filled out by one of the judges might appears as follows:

**STATE BAND CONTEST
ARMSTRONG STADIUM
CENTRAL CITY, PENNSYLVANIA**

BAND: BLUE HILLS HIGH

	Maximum	Rating
Inspection	100	90
Music	300	240
Originality	100	100
Formations and Maneuvers	300	200
Spirit	100	50
Timing	100	100
	1,000	780

Comments by Judge:
Weak Point: Footwork, halts, lines, etc.
Strong Point: Musical attack, power, etc.

Judge: John Doe

6. Since the judges are located in different positions in the stadium and scoring all items independently, the scores will vary widely. For example, it is not unreasonable for scores for the formations and maneuvers of one unit to vary thus: first judge, 220; second judge, 130; third judge, 170; etc.

7. The scoring should not be related in any way to a unit's performance and score at a previous competition. Each competition has its special conditions which differ from those of every other. To illustrate:

a. Units perform at various times at different levels of proficiency.

b. Conditions such as audience, weather, field, and lighting vary.

c. Various judges score differently; some harshly, some leniently.

Announcing the winners   Several minutes after each entry has competed, each judge should have completed his score sheet for that entry. Following the contest, there will be one score sheet for each unit from each of the judges. These scores are then added. The winners should be announced in the following order: In third place, with a score of 3,720 points out of a possible 5,000: Red Mountain High. In second place, with a score of 4,055 points out of a possible 5,000: Green Valley High. In first place, with a score of 4,110 out of a possible 5,000: Westchester Estates High. Within one week the correspondence committee should send a copy of the entire competition scoring to each of the contestants.

Notes for the judges   1. Always score according to the proficiency level of the elements entered. It is suggested that just prior to the competition each unit should be presented to the audience with an announcement and then march down the field with music. This is the time to note the general level of proficiency involved.

2. Do not attempt to score anything except the inspection aspect until the unit's performance is 75 percent complete. Concentrate on the lines, music, maneuvers, originality, and spirit.

3. Be careful of rating the first unit to perform and using that rating as a yardstick to score the other contestants. Rate each unit by the general level of proficiency you set when the bands were introduced.

7

The uniform

SELECTING THE UNIFORM
When an organization is in the market for new uniforms the project should be undertaken with a dedicated effort. The first step is the formation of a committee of persons having suitable backgrounds for studying the situation and requirements in detail. A properly balanced selection committee would consist of:

1. The director
2. Two senior bandsmen of the unit
3. Two representatives of the sponsoring agency
4. A reputable clothing merchant who does not sell uniforms
5. A decorator or color expert
6. A qualified sketcher or artist

The committee should work out the problems here presented. The problems are many, and most of them are of a technical or semi-technical nature. They must be resolved to achieve the most satisfactory product. Usually any group discussing uniforms limits the talks to initial cost. This is an error and could be the reason why so many uniforms fail to meet the organization's total requirements. On the other hand, a very careful analysis of the problem will give a correct answer on uniforms and in many cases even reduce the cost. Since cost is such a varying factor, subject to budgets, etc., it cannot be treated as an item for analysis in this book.

Areas of concern in the selection of uniforms

1. Uniform design
2. The color factor
3. The weight of material and hats
4. The strength of material
5. The uniform cut or fit
6. A balanced uniform
7. A comfortable uniform
8. A healthy uniform
9. A distinctive uniform
10. A readily adaptable uniform
11. A less expensive, but high-quality uniform (This may sound paradoxical when considering only cloth and labor but not if the entire cost, i.e., cloth, labor, accouterments, etc., are weighed.)

The selection process

1. Uniform design

The specific factors that enter into a well-designed uniform, such as weight, color, and fit, are items that should be solved one by one and then altered slightly for the best end product. The complete uniform has many facets with very important roles; one of these is design.

When new uniforms are first mentioned, catalogues from several uniform companies should be requested. These will serve as reference material. The reference catalogue should be checked and notes made on the different features desired. Various questions on style or fashion will arise as the catalogues are studied. Decisions must be made as to whether or not the uniform will have:

    a. A high, medium, or low waist for the trousers
    b. Four, three, two, one, or no pockets in the trousers
    c. Slide fastener or button closing for the trousers
    d. Leg stripes or not
    e. A coat or a "battle jacket" type of top
    f. Narrow or wide collar on the jacket
    g. Visible or hidden belt
    h. One chest cross-belt or two
    i. Buttons, etc.

During the compilation of this list, about fifteen factors will become evident, all concerned with design. After the committee appraises these points and general agreement on the design features is reached, a group of sketches should be made. If the unit in question is a high school band, the art class can be of great assistance. Even if the unit considering the uniforms is not a part of the high school, the art students might still aid the group by submitting sketches of uniforms. The art class must be given a list of the specifications decided upon, so that they can comply with these requirements when preparing the sketches. During the preparation and evaluation of the design sketches, every consideration should be given to the historical background and geographical location of the organization. For example, the wearing of a sea-going uniform by the Dismal Seepage Desert High band is rather incongruous. When the sketches have been submitted for appraisal, there should be a committee meeting for the purpose of evaluating, eliminating, and changing the drawings. During the evaluation the committee should eliminate the undesirable sketches and retain a maximum of three good ones, which presumably include all the desirable features. These three sketches should be stenciled and enough mimeograph copies obtained to permit further evaluation and final selection of design by the committee.

2. The color factor

After resolving the design of the uniform the committee must proceed to the second vital element. A critical aspect of visual appearance is color. The correct color combination can be appealing or eye-catching, but to be so the combinations cannot be a smear. Some of the combinations of color that can be seen in band uniforms include:

    a. Orange, trimmed with white or yellow
    b. Light red, trimmed with yellow or blue
    c. Light blue, trimmed with white
    d. Dark red, trimmed with black

These color and trim matchings present a rather poor appearance because of the combination—they do not show good contrast. Some color combinations in uniforms are so poor that even at a short distance there is no clear-cut appearance. A blending of colors is not distinctive. The single band uniform should be distinctive and, in addition, when the entire band is assembled, it should still retain its distinctiveness. A homogeneous mass of colors can be expensive, but may not achieve the purpose the buyers visualized. A uniform designed on the following color scheme will result in a homogeneous mass:

- a. A light blue uniform
- b. White stripes on the trousers
- c. As many as ten white, one-half-inch stripes across the tunic
- d. White citation cord
- e. Bright colored epaulettes
- f. White figures on the coat sleeve cuffs
- g. White waist belt
- h. Large hat with blue or white plumes
- i. All kinds of decorative buttons
- j. Cross-belts, etc.

A band fitted with uniforms so colored and moving at a distance of fifty yards approximates indistinguishability because of the cluttering blend. The band becomes a homogeneous mass, and yet such uniforms are usually quite expensive because of all of the accouterments, the extra labor involved, etc. (A diamond mixed with broken glass becomes invisible, but on a piece of black velvet it is a thing of beauty.) The color trim on any basic uniform color should be held to a minimum and should be a definite contrast, not a blend.

A few color combinations that are very distinctive and show contrast, if they are not too cluttered with extras, are as follows:

Basic Color	Trim
Dark to medium blue	White
Black	White or light green
White	Red or dark green
Dark to medium green	White

Red and blue, in that order, have the least resistance to fading, i.e., they lose color faster when exposed to light than do any other shades. Shades of yellow, orange, and purple for basic uniform colors give some degree of a smear effect when contrasted with most backgrounds.

Another color factor that should be considered is the average temperature in which the uniform will be worn versus the basic color of the uniform. It is a well-known fact that the darker the color, the more heat it will absorb. A general rule might be this: In warm sections of the country, select light tones for the basic color and darker colors for the trim. Conversely, in colder sections the basic color should be dark and the trim light. All such considerations must be weighed in the correct manner to assure the maximum comfort obtainable for the bandsman in uniform.

A color factor that should be given a very important place in the planning of uniforms is that of the shoes. A major violation of distinctive coloring is evident when a unit appears with white shoes, two-tone browns, blacks, reds, or even loafers. The discussion of shoe color introduces another important factor concerning footwear. A white shoe contrasts to a maximum degree with green grass or city streets; therefore, unless the unit is extremely adept in footwork, white shoes, spats, and in the same vein, light stripes on trousers, should be avoided. These contrasting colors emphasize footwork and exaggerate errors. The best color for shoes is black because it complements most uniforms and does not draw attention to errors. It blends with the street or grass and this is the one instance in which a blend with the environment is desirable unless, of course, the unit can boast of outstanding footwork. Black shoes will complement any uniform color except brown or tan, unless the tan has a gray or silver cast. Brown shoes will complement any straight brown or tan basic color.

3. Weight of material

The weight of the uniform plays an important part in the bandsman's comfort and proficiency. Many uniforms might be compared to a matted quilt. They are heavy and uncomfortable. If the temperature averages about 35 degrees each time the band performs, then it would be wise to select a heavy uniform, but the average performance is given in weather that is far above the freezing point. A heavy, matted uniform cannot be lightened. If the uniforms are a medium weight and have an open weave which allows the body to breathe, they will be comfortable and healthy in warm weather work. As the weather becomes cooler the individual member can wear extra clothes underneath the uniform, i.e., pajamas or anything that common sense dictates. Two light layers of clothing offer much more protective insulation than one heavy layer. The entrapped air layers are excellent insulators. However, the usual approach to the problem is to buy a uniform that is heavy enough for the coldest weather instead of one that would be comfortable in the average temperature for the area.

The weave of a uniform also plays a major role because a light-weight material can be woven almost airtight and therefore become a sweatbox. Following are suggestions for uniform materials.

Specifications for cloth weight and weave.
    a. Heavy uniforms—wool
        (1) Cloth weight: 12 ounces, minimum
                               16 ounces, maximum
        (2) Weave: gabardine or serge
    b. Light uniforms—cotton
        (1) Cloth weight: 5 ounces, minimum
                               8 ounces, maximum

(2) Weave: the highest porosity in cotton without sacrificing strength is about 45 CPM. (This is a manufacturer's specification meaning that for a given area of the cloth, air under specified pressure can be forced through at 45 cubic feet per minute.)

Cotton and wool fibers have very minute hairs sticking out along their entire length. These can be seen on a single fiber if magnified. These minute hairs keep the main fiber from resting on the body or against underclothing. The space thus provided is an insulating air space, which not only resists temperature changes, but allows the body to breathe freely. The clammy or eerie sensation created by many

Diagram 57 / **Uniform headgear**

synthetic fibered cloths is due to the absence of the minute hairs along the fibers. The fiber is smooth and, therefore, lies directly against the body, thus eliminating the insulating air space and retarding proper breathing of the body (skin).

4. Hats for the uniform

When discussing the weight of uniforms it is essential to consider the headgear worn by the musicians. Much of the cost of the total uniform may be attributed to the price of the hat selected. Many are heavy, hard to balance, airtight, and uncomfortable. A comfortable hat should be a goal set by the committee. A few guidelines are as follows:

a. A light and comfortable, yet very smart hat is one with a short bill, high front, and soft flexible head rim with a total weight of approximately six and one half ounces. See *Diagram 57*.

b. The lightest and least expensive is a cloth hat known as the service "overseas" hat, which has a total weight of approximately one and one half ounces. See *Diagram 58*.

c. The absolute maximum weight should never be more than nine ounces. When above nine ounces, hats are too heavy, usually rigid, and therefore, uncomfortable. Anything that makes a bandsman uncomfortable reduces his efficiency.

d. As important as the weight of a hat is to comfort, research has proven that another factor is equally important. That factor is ventilation. Proper ventilation can be achieved in the billed type hat by an open-weave sideband or by numerous eyelets or "air holes" on

Diagram 58 / **Uniform headgear**

the underside of the crown. The avenues for air access coupled with a soft top which will move up and down slightly as the person walks simulates a miniature bellows, taking in and exhausting air continually with movement.

e. Pompons add cost and weight to the hat but little else. The hats described in a. and b. above are healthful, comfortable, and inexpensive. All musical marching units could be equipped with each type; they can be used alternately to give the unit a fresh appearance or as the occasion demands.

5. Strength of material

It is a case of penny wise and pound foolish to purchase uniforms fabricated from inferior material. No matter how concentrated the efforts of the leaders may be in attempting to prevent it, the uniform undergoes some fairly severe strains in ordinary and perhaps extraordinary usage. In addition to the wear and tear by the bandsman, the uniform is subjected to multiple cleanings. In the specifications covering new uniforms, the requirement for all seams to be strongly stitched and of a locked stitch type that will not unravel should be emphasized. During the process of uniform selection, due to the natural excitement of obtaining new colors and designs, it is easy to understand that on occasion the strength factor may be overlooked. Such an oversight must be guarded against in every selection. This is another obvious reason for selecting a good committee to work on the problem. The reputable clothing merchant or tailor who is a member of the committee can study this problem and guard against such misfortunes. Further, it is a good idea to have a clause covering the "minimum life" of the material inserted into the contract. Such a clause will protect the buyer from purchasing an inferior material, and it likewise will alert the manufacturer to the seriousness of the problem and the necessity of supplying a good product.

On some occasions even good material will deteriorate in one-half of the lifetime expected of it, due to misuse and neglect of the uniforms. No cotton or woolen fabric can be used repeatedly and soaked with highly corrosive perspiration and long remain in good condition. Not only does perspiration stain material, but it also decays the material quite rapidly. A rigid routine should be followed concerning the cleaning and airing of the uniform. Any time, for example, that the uniform becomes soaked with perspiration, it should be aired thoroughly and then cleaned. When it must be used before cleaning because of close commitments, the uniform should be aired thoroughly for approximately two hours. This is not only a sanitary measure, but also prolongs the life of the fabric. If the uniforms are stored in a common area near the practice room, then their care could be monitored by the unit manager or supply man. However, if the uniform is to be handed to each man as an individual responsibility, a mimeographed sheet of instructions, as to its care, should accompany it. In the case of high school bands or bands composed of even younger members, the "Instructions for the Care of Uniforms" should be sent to the home of each member.

6. Uniform cut or fit

An area for noticeable improvement of the bandsman's appearance is the uniform cut or fit. Ceremonial guard units or special show teams select men whose heights are between six feet and six feet two and who are also well proportioned. The selection is made to obtain maximum uniformity, which is a great asset to a show unit. The situation facing the director of a musical marching unit is entirely different from that facing the leader of a ceremonial guard. To form a band, the director must select persons with from three to ten years' training who can play the instruments required. Consequently, unless the director has an endless number of prospective members from which to choose, he must deal with all sizes and shapes of players. The one means the director has for obtaining some degree of uniformity is that of disguising the differences in size and shape with the uniform the unit members wear.

Many uniforms are cut to fit like a wet bathing suit on a model; but a band of sixty musicians is not made up of perfect forms. It does not matter whether it is a high school band or a V.F.W. drum and bugle corps composed entirely of veterans, the size problem remains. Some of the members may be tall and fat; some short and fat. Some may be tall and thin, others are medium in height, etc. Size is most obvious in any person when he is wearing a very close fitting garment. Tall members appear taller and the stout members appear stouter. Instead of striving for uniformity, which is after all what a uniform attempts to depict, the tight-fitting uniform accomplishes just the opposite—it accents nonuniformity. The committee should keep this in mind and endeavor to de-emphasize differences in build by partially concealing them in the uniform cut. Instead of having a skin-fitting ensemble, the tunic, blouse, or battle jacket should be loose. This means larger sleeves so that the folds of the sleeves are not dictated by rolls of flesh underneath, etc. A jacket that fits the chest comfortably, not like a corset, but as a summer sport coat or jacket, is desirable. The optimum design is a semi-drape coat or jacket. The trousers, likewise, should not be skin-tight or have tight belts, etc. In addition to achieving a greater degree of uniformity the cuts recommended are more healthful, comfortable, and economical because:

  a. The body can breathe easier.

  b. The tailoring is not too expensive and elaborate.

  c. A slight shrinkage of uniforms or the weight variation of a bandsman will not render the apparel useless.

  d. The adaptability to another bandsman is facilitated.

7. Balanced uniforms

By this time it should be obvious that the matter of selecting new uniforms must be a long-range program worked out in detail, not merely an act of pointing to a specific uniform in a catalogue. The factors for consideration are numerous and they should be analyzed and resolved individually and collectively before the final specifications are written.

Two general designs which adequately incorporate all of the desirable factors discussed follow. See *Diagram 59.*

  a. The cool weather uniform

(1) Design

    (a) The battle-type jacket has the advantages of firm appearance. With a blouse-type coat, the loose bottom is always in motion due to a blowing wind or body movement. This motion tends to make the individual member and/or the entire unit appear unstable. The battle jacket embraces the following features:

    1 Neat appearance under operating conditions.

    2 A zippered (slide fastener) front.

    3 Two fake breast pockets.

    4 Wide, open collar.

    5 Wide, full lapels.

    6 Epaulettes as part of the jacket and the same color as that of the jacket.

    7 A one-inch-wide band on each cuff.

    8 Neat fit but by no means tight.

    (b) Plain-style trousers of the color used in the jacket which embrace the following features:

    1 A very high rise (commonly called waistband) so that the jacket does not creep up above the trousers no matter what position a man might assume in the execution of his task with the unit.

    2 One heavy-duty, zippered inside pocket in front but hidden inside the waist band in order to carry a wallet or loose money.

Diagram 59 / **Cool weather uniform**

3 No side pockets because, when present, these are usually loaded and present unsightly bulges.

4 One rear pocket in which to carry a folded handkerchief.

5 Strong suspender buttons—no belt loops. Suspenders keep the pants neat and in shape, whereas a belt does not necessarily do so.

6 A heavy zippered front with a positive zipper lock.

7 No leg stripes.

8 No cuffs.

9 The trouser bottoms should slope slightly to the back (approximately one-fourth inch) and should incorporate a fabric reinforcement or guard at the back to prevent abrasion by the shoe heel.

(c) For accouterments the bare essentials are:

1 A full scarf which permits easy breathing and will also cover any garment worn underneath the jacket. There are scarves now on the market that are ready tied and fasten by a clip at the back of the neck. These look best when new because of the uniform tie but they are difficult to clean. If the flat type of scarf that must be tied is used, then instructions on tying are necessary to achieve uniformity.

2 A two-and-one-half-inch waist belt of whipcord which fastens by eyes and hooks to the jacket. This belt does not support anything—it is merely a dress accessory. The buckle can be chromium or brass, this selection to be determined by uniform colors. For example, with a white trim a chromium buckle should be used. This waist belt and buckle are optional since they are really not necessary.

3 A single cross-belt of a similar size and material which snaps to the jacket underneath the belt on the left side of the waist. This cross-belt does not support anything—it is merely for dress therefore it is an optional item.

(d) For the hat, see *Diagram 57*.

(e) Black high-gloss shoes are excellent.

(2) Color

A medium dark blue for the basic color and white for the trim color because of contrast. Of course, there are many good combinations that can be used. These combinations to a large extent will be dictated by the colors of the organization.

(3) Weight of material

This factor must be carefully determined by climatic conditions peculiar to the area of operation. However, it should be kept in mind that most uniforms are made of material that is too heavy and with too close a weave.

(4) Uniform cut or fit

Although the uniform illustrated looks neat, it is possible for it to do much toward concealing the true figure of the wearer if the uniform is not tight. It is designed with the idea of wearing additional clothing underneath when and if necessary.

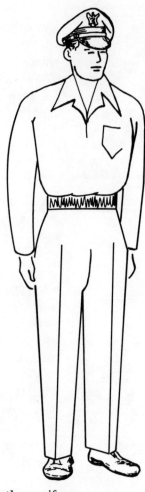

Diagram 60 / **Warm weather uniform**

b. The warm weather uniform

The second design is of a warm weather uniform which balances uniformity, distinctiveness, and comfort. See *Diagram 60.*

(1) Design

(a) A very light weight slipover-type shirt with a light-weight basket weave waistband is quite acceptable. This waistband must not be tight. The shirt embraces the following features:

1 Constructed of lightweight, wide mesh cotton; wash-and-wear type is fine.

2 Very light blue body color with a dark blue collar. The color of the collar should match that of the trousers.

3 Wide, open neckline for maximum ventilation.

4 One fake breast pocket.

5 Full cut, even to the extent of being considered slightly billowy.

(b) The trousers should be a medium to dark blue color. The trousers embrace the following features:

1 Constructed of lightweight cotton with a wide or open mesh, however not to the extent of being transparent; wash-and-wear type is fine.

2 A high rise.

3 Suspender buttons, but no belt loops.

4 A front pocket concealed inside the waistband that is large enough to carry a wallet. This pocket should be of heavy material and zippered across the top.

5 No side pockets.

6 One rear pocket for carrying a folded handkerchief.

7 No leg stripes.

8 Heavy zippered front with positive zipper lock.

9 No cuffs.

(c) No accouterments whatsoever are necessary since the difference in color between the shirt and trousers will give enough dress to the unit.

(d) With the warm weather uniform either of the types of hat shown can be worn. The shoes should be black and capable of taking a high-gloss finish.

(2) Color

A very light pastel blue is ideal for the shirt and a medium blue for the trousers. In the warm weather uniform, there are many more alternates for color combinations than there are with the cool weather uniform. A word of advice on this subject is to keep the shirt or upper section of the uniform a lighter color than the bottom or trousers in order to prevent the organization from looking top-heavy.

(3) Weight of material

The material should be very lightweight and constructed with a wide weave to promote maximum ventilation and easy body breathing.

(4) Uniform cut or fit

The fit should be as loose as possible without having the appearance of a misfit.

The idea of two uniforms may seem like an extravagant procedure to the sponsors; but, disregarding all the benefits to the organization itself, in most cases the two uniforms discussed will cost no more than one of the type now in use. Cleaning or laundering the two types illustrated is much less expensive than for the overdecorated type and, in addition, all accouterments are removable for individual cleaning, which eliminates all chance of fading, etc.

The problem of uniform procurement should be planned, investigated, and finally terminated as one of far-reaching consequence because, in essence, it is just that.

Uniforms and temperature ranges

The proper uniform-temperature range combination should always be considered. Recommendations for the correct clothing for a particular temperature range are at most rules of thumb, since humidity and wind complicate the comfort range:

1. With temperatures ranging from 20 to 35 degrees Fahrenheit, the cool weather uniform with a set of pajamas, or an equivalent, underneath can be worn.

2. With temperatures ranging from 35 to 60 degrees Fahrenheit, the cool weather uniform can be worn.

3. With temperatures ranging upward from 60 degrees the warm weather uniform can be worn.

advanced footwork   Special footwork that spans two categories. First, it is absolutely necessary in many cases for precision footwork. Second, it can be used to add a high degree of flash to footwork.

accouterment   An accessory for an instrument or a uniform; trumpet banner and cross-belts for the uniforms are accouterments.

band   A marching musical unit.

block and block formation   The terms are used interchangeably. The block is the assembly formation or the straight marching formation of the unit. The block is identified by the number of ranks and files it contains. A block of twelve ranks and eight files contains ninety-six men.

box reverse   A precision maneuver that reverses the direction of the unit 180 degrees and allows it to retain its original orientation as to flanks and guide. The box reverse can be executed on an area no larger than that required by the block formation.

chain of command   The line of authority in an organization. The understanding, in an organization, that certain problems will be handled by specified individuals who have been granted specific authorities and responsibilities. The authority and responsibility vested in the third trumpet section head is small but grows greater in the trumpet section head, brass section head, and so on.

committee   A group of persons organized on a functional basis to accomplish some specific task.

committee leader   The ranking man on each committee. It is difficult, if not impossible, for a committee leader to supervise directly more than ten persons.

coordinators   Persons with complete information and assistance during a parade or field competition. They are not at the command posts.

command line   The route or passage of instructions, orders, etc., within the chain of command of an organization.

command of execution   The command following the preparatory command. It designates the time or step on which the action will begin.

command post   The physical location of the coordinators at the time of the event.

diagonal   In the strict sense this is any line that intersects two parallel lines at any angle other than 90 degrees; for marching units the diagonal means 45 degrees only.

drum corps   A marching musical unit.

epaulet or **epaulette**   A shoulder ornament worn on uniforms

established interval   A distance corresponding to two established paces.

established pace   The average pace of the unit determined by an exact procedure.

file A row of persons (musicians) arranged one behind the other. The files are parallel to the direction of march. At times a file may be called a column.

file cover The act of keeping the file a straight projection.

file guide Means used to keep the file covered or straight. File guide is always straight ahead.

filewise Term indicating action by a file.

flanks (1) 90-degree turns; (2) the outside files of the unit.

fundamental footwork The basic footwork absolutely necessary to march and maneuver any unit.

guide system A method of maintaining the established intervals and alignment of a marching unit.

guide T An imaginary T set in the block formation. The head of the T acts as the lead element in guiding the files; it also sets the intervals within ranks. The head of the T is the front rank. The stem of the T acts as the lead element in guiding the ranks; it also sets the intervals within files to the established intervals. The stem of the T is a file.

homogeneous mass A blend or confusion of too much color and too many accessories rendering the whole a rather indistinguishable mass from relatively short distances.

I.P. Initial point, the point beyond the assembly area at which the parade officially begins. The I.P. is the "start here point" where the units pick up their correct parade column spacing and step off with music. The I.P. should be plainly designated in each parade .

interval The space separating two marchers. The word is descriptive when used with a designation such as "the interval between men in a rank," which means the right and/or left distance to the next man, lateral distance; the interval between men in a file means the distance ahead and/or behind to the next man. The intervals in the head of the T determine the intervals between the files; the intervals in the stem of the T determine the intervals between the ranks.

marching musical unit Any musical organization which plays music while on the march: a fife and drum corps, a pipe band, a drum and bugle corps, a high school or college band, etc.

military commander In this book, commander of a military post, station, or base to whom the band leader is responsible.

maximum flexible strength The operating strength of the unit. Contains sufficient strength that any vacancies in the block may be filled for any operation.

nonsymmetrical formation Any formation that does not have two identical halves.

oblique An angle of 45 degrees (as used in this book).

pace The established step in march.

pacesetter The one person in the marching unit responsible for maintaining the established pace of the entire unit. In a T guide system, this individual is located where the stem and head of the T intersect.

pacing limits The length of stride that can be maintained with comfort and precision. The pacing limit can be under- or overshot, since too short a pace will render precision marching an impossibility just as much as too long a pace.

parade column The sequencing and spacing of the elements in a parade.

parade route The path the parade column will march during the parade.

precision Exactness, the quality of sharpness.

preparatory command The order describing the action to be taken upon the command of execution.

procurement Acquisition. The act of obtaining supplies.

quick time 120 to 130 steps per minute

rank A formation of men abreast of each other. In block formation a rank is perpendicular to the block formation's direction of march, while a file is parallel to its direction of march. At times the rank may be called a line.

rank cover The act of keeping the rank a straight projection.

rank guide Means used to keep the rank covered or straight. Rank guide is either right or left, depending upon which side of the rank guide the man is positioned. The rank guides are in the stem of the T.

rankwise Term indicating action by a rank.

section head A person appointed to have secondary control, after the director, of a group of men engaged in similar activities; for example, the section head for percussion.

show formation A formation designed to be presented to the public for a special occasion or event. A formation is a pictorial still. An example is the longhorn steer described in this book.

show maneuver A maneuver emphasizes movement as the principle aspect of the work. An example is operation scatter.

SOP Standard operating procedure.

symmetrical formation A formation that can be divided into two equal halves, one half being the mirror image of the other half.

T (see **guide T** and **guide system**)

time of execution The time or step on which the designated action begins. This is the step following the step on which the command of execution is given.

unit A musical marching organization.

unit commander As used here, it means the person commanding the unit at the time the activity being described is taking place. One from whom the unit is taking orders for that particular phase of its operations. This person may be at times the director, drill master, drum major, or any other designated leader who is controlling the activities of the unit for some special activity.

visual balance A balance of instrumentation in each rank, a symmetrical sizing in each rank according to height.